COMPUTER J EXPLAINED

by Nicholas Enticknap

ComputerWeekly

Published by Computer Weekly Publications
Quadrant House, Sutton, Surrey, SM2 5AS

Publications Manager: John Riley
Publications Executive: Robin Frampton
Publications Assistant: Katherine Canham

REED
BUSINESS
PUBLISHING © 1989

British Library Cataloguing in Publication Data

Enticknap, Nicholas
  Computer jargon explained. – 2nd ed.
  1. Computer Systems
  I. Title II. Enticknap, Nicholas. Breaking the jargon.
  004

ISBN 1 85384 015 7

All rights reserved. No part of the publication may be reproduced, stored in a retrieval system or transmitted, in any form or by any means, electronic, mechanical, photocopying, recording and/or otherwise, without the prior written permission of the publishers.

Disc conversion and typesetting by Columns of Reading
Printed in England

CONTENTS

Introduction	1
Ada	3
Analyst workbench	5
Artificial intelligence	7
Case (Computer-aided software engineering)	9
CCITT	11
Cim (Computer integrated manufacturing)	13
Cmos/ECL	16
Cycle time	18
Database	21
Data dictionary	24
Data protection	26
Design methodologies	28
Desktop publishing	30
Distributed database	32
EDI	34
Esprit	36
Ethernet	38
Expert system	39
Fault tolerance	41
Fifth generation	43
File server	45
Fourth generation language	46
Function point	48
Gallium arsenide	50
Ipse (Integrated project support environment)	52
ISDN	54
ISO	56
Lan (Local area network)	58
LU 6.2	60
Mainframe, mini, micro	62
Mainframe generations	65
Map/Top	67
Mercury	68
Mips (Millions of instructions per second)	70

NCC	73
Non-procedural language	75
ODA	77
Office automation	79
Optical computing	82
Optical disc	84
Optical fibre	87
OSI	89
Parallel processing	90
Pick	93
Protocol	95
Relational database	96
Risc (Reduced instruction set computer)	98
SAA	100
SNA	102
Spreadsheet	104
SQL	105
Superconductivity	107
Teletex	110
Thin-film head	112
Token ring	113
Unix	115
Vans (Value-added network service)	117
VDU standards	118
Vector processing	120
Vertical recording	122
Videotex	124
VLSI	126
von Neumann architecture	128
Wafer scale integration	130
Workstation	133
X.25	135
X.400	137
X-Stream	138
Appendix 1 – Abbreviations: technical terms	140
Appendix 2 – Abbreviations: organisations	154
Appendix 3 – Units of measure	159
Index	162

INTRODUCTION

Computer jargon has a bad name. It irritates non-computer people: it causes problems for computer people. The technology and the industry are changing so rapidly it is very hard even for professionals to keep up to date.

Computer people have to concentrate on the problems in hand: they do not have time to keep abreast of developments that do not immediately affect what they are doing. Nonetheless, they are expected to be experts: to have instant, detailed, accurate answers to every question a non-specialist may pose them.

This book provides the solution for computer professionals who need that wider perspective. It discusses 68 of the most commonly used technical computing terms. In each case it explains what the term means: in addition, it explains why the term is important to the computer professional, and how it relates to the trends and developments which are driving the information technology industry.

The book is the brainchild of Nicholas Enticknap, a former computer professional and now established as one of the leading commentators on computer industry developments. It is based on a series of articles he wrote for *Computer Weekly* under the heading *Background Briefing*. The series, which appeared in instalments between November 1986 and January 1989, has been brought up to date and expanded with three appendices and a comprehensive index.

ADA

Is there such a thing as an ideal programming language, suitable for all types of application?

This Holy Grail has been sought by a large number of computer scientists over the years, some of whom have been quite convinced they have found it.

Algol was probably the first language for which this universality of application was claimed. Not long afterwards, IBM introduced PL/I which was said to combine the virtues of Cobol and Fortran within a single language. More recently, APL has also had its enthusiastic proponents.

None of these languages has hit the target as far as the majority of users are concerned. PL/I is in fairly widespread use thanks to its IBM backing, but Cobol and Fortran have remained overwhelmingly the most popular languages, while Basic has assumed much the same position among PC users.

Ada has been put forward by its supporters as another claimant for the role. This is rather more than its instigator, the US Department of Defense, claims: its intention was specifically to produce a language suitable for programming embedded systems.

Embedded systems are a type of real time process control system used in aircraft, tanks, destroyers and the like, where fast and reliable real time response to situations which are dynamically changing in a mathematically complex way is the norm.

A number of such languages exist, and the DoD could have standardised on one of them. It decided not to, principally because none of the candidates met its requirements for reliability of use coupled with ease and economy of maintenance.

This requirement dictated a new approach to programming language design, and Ada is significant because it stimulated new thinking which has now become an integral part of software engineering theory.

In particular, it recognises that errors in software systems frequently arise because of the size of the system and therefore its complexity, making it impossible for any one person to hold the whole scheme in their head.

Thus Ada embodies the principle of a modular systems structure to an extent that individual parts of programs can be separately compiled, and linked together afterwards.

More importantly, it recognises that coding is only part of the systems design process. Ada is not only a language, it is also a set of tools supporting every part of the systems design process.

This idea of a programming support environment has now become, independently of Ada itself, an integral part of fifth generation thinking.

A key characteristic of Ada is that it is standardised. To be acceptable by the DoD, an Ada compiler must pass a validation procedure designed by the Ada Joint Program Office (AJPO) to ensure that it does meet the standard.

AJPO was set up by the DoD to implement its own requirements. Its validation procedures are now accepted by other procurement bodies such as the British Ministry of Defence.

The same standardisation is true in principle of the Ada project support environment (Apse). However, AJPO has not yet issued a validation suite for Apses, and in practice there are two different apses in use with Ada. One is Cais (Common apse interface set), supported by the DoD; the other is PCTE (Portable Common Tools Environment), preferred by European countries. There are significant differences between the two, and efforts are currently being made to bring them closer together.

The specification for Ada was completed in 1979, and the first compilers appeared in 1983. The DoD standardised on use of the language in 1985, and the MoD followed suit in 1987. By the end of 1987 there were just under 150 validated compilers on the market.

Ada is not an acronym. The name was chosen to honour Lady Ada Lovelace, assistant to Charles Babbage, who is credited with being the world's first programmer.

ANALYST WORKBENCH

Program maintenance is a major problem for every computer installation. Some is unavoidable, due to changes in the business environment. Most of the rest stems from mistakes made in the development process, and a large part of that is due to poor systems analysis.

The industry has tackled this problem by concentrating on developing automated tools for programmers, such as interactive development tools and fourth generation languages. Until recently there has, in contrast, been little progress made in helping analysts.

With the advent of computer-aided design (Cad) systems for engineers, however, it was recognised that computer power could equally be applied to help systems analysts. Thus was born the concept of the analyst workbench.

Workbenches, like Cad workstations, consist of graphics terminals equipped with special-purpose software. They automate the tasks carried out during analysis, allowing analysts to construct diagrams on the screen, and to gather information about the data elements involved in the task being analysed. Automatic validation facilities are provided to detect errors and ambiguities, which can then be resolved on the spot with the user.

Analyst workbenches can be stand-alone, but are more commonly used as part of a total automated development environment. This allows new systems to be integrated with existing ones during the development process, preventing duplication and thus another rich source of errors. It also allows automatic code generation to become the end result of the analysis process, raising the prospect of the elimination of the programming process altogether.

The first workbenches appeared in the UK in 1985. Intech paved the way with Excelerator, which is today the most widely used product. ICL became one of the first mainframe manufacturers to release a workbench product with Quickbuild Workbench.

Others available include Automate from Learmonth & Burchett, Information Engineering Facility from James Martin Associates and Information Engineering Workbench from Arthur Young. The last two are designed to be used in conjunction with the information engineering methodology.

See also: Case design methodologies (page 28).

ARTIFICIAL INTELLIGENCE

Ever since the potential of machines first began to be realised in the 18th Century, man has dreamt of manufacturing man-like objects. As the technology changed so has the dream, and Frankenstein's monster of the early 19th Century had evolved into Asimov's robots by the time of the Second World War.

Then came the computer – popularly known in the early days as the "electronic brain" – and the dream looked set to become a reality. Researchers around the world started trying to translate science fiction into science fact, and the new academic discipline was christened "artificial intelligence" in 1956.

Several benefits could be seen from a machine which could emulate the intelligent thought processes of a human being without suffering from human frailty and fallibility. There were cost savings to be made in commercial enterprises, and competitive advantages to be had in Government and military circles.

This was incentive enough to ensure funding was forthcoming, but for a couple of decades there was little tangible progress and the sceptics gained the upper hand. In the UK, the Government-sponsored Lighthill Report of the early 1970s was highly pessimistic about the potential of artificial intelligence, and severely inhibited research here for 10 years or more.

Broadly speaking, the drive to develop artificial intelligence has been carried out in two ways. The first was to study the thought and judgment processes of human beings, and then attempt to describe them in ways which could form a basis for the development of computer programs.

This ambitious attempt to create from scratch a sound theoretical basis for artificial intelligence work has produced disappointing results so far (hence the temporary triumph of the sceptics). The alternative far more pragmatic approach is beginning to produce some notable successes (hence the current growing interest in the subject).

The pragmatic approach starts with the computer and steadily attempts to make it more human-like. The passage of time has helped greatly, as more computing power and memory have become available for the same money.

Chess-playing computers provide a measure of the progress made. Only 10 years ago their playing standard was very elementary, and any half-way competent player could beat them easily. Today, the best chess-playing systems can give international masters a good game, and the day is in sight when the first victory over a grandmaster will be registered.

Of more practical value is the application of artificial intelligence techniques in the pursuit of user-friendliness. Natural language database front-ends such as AIC's Intellect and Cullinet's On-Line English are examples of what can be achieved today, and fifth generation computers will certainly embody similar techniques far more extensively.

Probably the best-known commercial spin-off from artificial intelligence work is the expert system. This has emerged from a sub-discipline of artificial intelligence known as knowledge engineering, the key to which is a recognition that human thinking is as much dependent on the possession of knowledge as on the ability to reason.

Knowledge engineering is thus the specialist study of the task of transferring knowledge from a human expert to a computer program.

Today, therefore, artificial intelligence techniques are helping to make computers both more useful and more usable. In the next decade they are expected to become an essential part of all systems design. But, although Asimov's robots have now been replaced by Arthur C Clarke's HAL, the initial dream remains as far from being realised as ever.

See also: Expert system (page 39).

8

CASE (COMPUTER-AIDED SOFTWARE ENGINEERING)

Once computers started to be widely used, it quickly became apparent that control procedures for software development left much to be desired.

Projects invariably took longer than expected and cost more than had been budgeted. The programs produced were far from reliable. Maintaining them was a complex task, fraught with difficulty if, as was often the case, the original programmer had left.

Dissatisfaction with these limitations of the systems development process prompted the academics to put on their thinking caps. One line of thought that emerged held that the desired improvements could be effected by applying the control principles used in engineering to the software life cycle. This led to the coining of the term "software engineering" in 1968.

The term won acceptance in academic circles at once, and has since become more widespread. The job position "software engineer" began to appear in the seventies, and is now common in the computer industry, particularly among mini and micro suppliers.

The National Computing Centre now offers a basic certificate in software engineering course, analogous to its established and respected course for systems analysts. The first students to complete the nine-week course graduated in 1988.

Throughout the seventies, software engineering was concerned with the development and application of methodologies that could be applied to the development process.

In the eighties, there emerged a class of products designed to apply computer power to the process of systems development, in the same way as workstations apply computer power to the process of engineering design. It seemed natural to call these new products computer-aided software engineering (Case) tools.

There is no hard-and-fast definition of a Case tool. The term is used to embrace products which automate part of the programming function (such as fourth generation languages), the analysis function (workbenches) and the entire systems development process (integrated project support environments).

The Government has initiated two schemes to publicise the use of Case tools. First, it has funded the establishment of a Software Tools Demonstration Centre in Manchester. The Centre, which opened early in 1987, provides prospective users with details of 35 tools for streamlining each stage of software development.

Second, it has set up the Software Engineering Demonstration Initiative. This is designed to create a fund of publicly available knowledge in the use of Case tools. It works by sponsoring a number of end-users to use Case tools in real-life demonstration projects.

See also: Analyst workbench (page 15), Design methodologies (page 28), and Ipse (page 52).

CCITT

A number of bodies formulate standards which affect computer installations. One of the best known is the CCITT, which develops standards affecting all forms of public telecommunication, including telephony, telex and fax as well as data communications.

The CCITT is the representative body of the world's public telecomms administrations (normally referred to as PTTs, the letters standing for Post, Telephone and Telegraph). These bodies may be national monopolies (as the Post Office once was in the UK), or privately owned companies (such as British Telecom and AT&T).

Various other bodies are involved in the CCITT standards-making process, such as manufacturers, users and other organisations with an interest in the outcome. Their role is purely advisory and they have no vote.

The standards made by the CCITT are put forward as "recommendations". As they are formulated by PTTs, however, and adopted without question by them, they are more rigorously adhered to than almost any other type of standard. The CCITT's achievements have been most impressive in the fields of telephony, telex and fax, though so far less so in data communications.

This is principally because data communications is still a new field, and is far more complex than the earlier forms of telecommunication. Nonetheless, the CCITT has had its successes here too.

Among the most notable is the V.24 standard, which describes the interface for connecting a terminal to a modem. This interface (also known as RS232) has been widely adopted for many other uses, particularly connecting peripherals such as VDUs and printers to computer processors.

The X series packet-switching standards (of which X.25 is the most often quoted) has also gained an impressive degree of acceptance among computer manufacturers as well as among PTTs.

Less successful have been the teletex standards (F.200 describing the service, and a set of T series standards specifying hardware requirements). This work, intended to provide a basis for a telex-replacement international document transmission service, was completed in 1980, but teletex has obstinately refused to take off since.

For the record, the letters CCITT stand for Comite Consultatif Internationale de Telegraphique et Telephonique. The organisation is constituted as a part of the International Telecommunications Union and is headquartered in Geneva.

CIM (COMPUTER-INTEGRATED MANUFACTURING)

During the early part of the computer revolution, when companies everywhere were computerising their administrative procedures, manufacturing applications were more or less ignored. Since then, computers have been applied to manufacturing applications in three areas which have until recently remained largely independent of each other.

The first class of application was the "back-office" tasks needed to ensure a factory runs efficiently. These include material requirements planning (MRP), capacity planning and purchasing. They have traditionally been run on mainframes.

At around the same time, in the mid-sixties, computers began to be used for automating factory processes. This involved the invention of a new type of system, the minicomputer, which was capable of providing responses to information gathered from sensors in real time, and could be packaged into factory machinery.

Process control was not itself a new concept. Since the forties, machine tools had operated under the control of punched tapes which specified numeric parameters such as position. Such machines were known as numerically controlled (NC) machines.

Originally these parameters were calculated by engineers manually. With the arrival of the computer that task could be offloaded, and the concept of the computer numerically-controlled (CNC) machine arrived.

A few years later, in the early seventies, computer and VDU technology had developed to the point where computer power became economic for use in the design office. Systems appeared which allowed engineers and architects to create designs on a screen, test them and modify them until satisfied. This took much of the labour out of drawing, and allowed designers to concentrate on the design process itself.

This technique became known as Cad (standing usually for computer-aided design, sometimes for computer-aided drafting).

For those manufacturing designs which subsequently went into production, it was logical to develop the facility for producing output which could be used as input to NC machines. Systems that could do this became known as Cad/Cam (with Cam standing for computer-aided manufacturing). Cam is an acronym which is rarely used separately.

Apart from this limited degree of integration, the three types of manufacturing application were run in isolation for many years, each developing along its own lines.

On the factory floor, process control became more widespread as the technology developed, the price/performance of minicomputers improved and the microcomputer arrived.

The major advance, however, was the advent of the robot, as this substantially increased the type of automation possible. Robots started to appear in British factories in the late seventies.

Cad systems also developed steadily over the years. The initial systems could construct drawings only in two dimensions and in black and white. Today we have 3D, colour and the additional facility for surface and solids modelling, doing away with the need for the designer to construct models in wood or clay.

Cad and Cad/Cam systems remained the province of large manufacturing organisations until the mid-eighties. At that stage the engineering workstation arrived, making Cad/Cam possible for a much larger number of companies. Since then, the arrival of the 32-bit PC has reduced the starting-price threshold still further.

About the same time, people began to realise that there were advantages in integrating the various types of separate computer-based manufacturing system. Most notably you could avoid entering data twice to two different applications, not only increasing efficiency but eliminating a major source of errors.

Companies that had a portfolio of manufacturing applications rapidly latched on to the concept, by building links between the separate products and selling the whole range under the name Cim (Computer-integrated manufacturing). Among the companies active in promoting the Cim concept were DEC, IBM, ICL, Prime and Unisys.

For users, however, the Cim concept, however desirable in theory, proved extremely difficult to implement in practice, and as a result Cim now has rather a bad name. The difficulty lay in connecting many different types of incompatible system.

Today Cim is recognised as something that will happen slowly, a bit at a time. The car manufacturers, which pioneered the use of robots, are also leading the way here.

The DTI announced its Advanced Manufacturing Technology Centre in 1985, to identify and solve problems in the use of manufacturing technology; to work with industry to get firms to exploit automation properly; and to train managers and staff to understand and apply the technology.

CMOS/ECL

The technology used in computer systems for both logic and memory circuits is almost entirely based on silicon (the exception is gallium-arsenide technology, which is found only in a small number of very high-powered systems). The silicon technologies fall into two major classes: Mos (standing for metal oxide semiconductor) and bipolar.

Each of these classes has a number of sub-classes, differing at a technical level and also in the properties they have. The major sub-classes in each type today are Cmos and ECL.

The 'C' in Cmos stands for Complementary, and refers to the way in which Cmos circuits are constructed from complementary pairs of transistors.

Cmos chips differ most significantly from other types of Mos chip in their unusually low power consumption. This first became valuable because it allowed batteries rather than the mains to be used as a power source, making Cmos an ideal technology for use in portable computers and terminals.

The pioneering portables used magnetic tape cassettes or cartridges, which are both bulkier and less reliable, or bubble memories, which are considerably more expensive.

The development of Cmos has provided an economical and compact alternative, and greatly stimulated the development of this market.

As time went on and Cmos technology evolved, it became possible to use it to construct larger computer processors. ICL led the way with the Series 39 Level 30 mainframe, launched in 1985. Today, most small processors are constructed from Cmos technology, including the Intel 80386 microprocessor used in many 32-bit personal computers.

The advantage in using Cmos in this type of system is that processors not only use very little power, but also dissipate very little heat, and can thus be used in normal office environments. The technology is also very compact, which reduces the demand for floor space.

There is a limit to how powerful a processor can be constructed from Cmos technology. Today, the most powerful Cmos processor available is the one used in the Unisys 200/400 mainframe announced in April 1988: this has a power rating of a little under 3 mips.

For more powerful systems, bipolar technology is used. The most common type of bipolar is ECL (standing for emitter-coupled logic). Another type that is widely used is TTL (standing for transistor-transistor logic).

ECL chips differ from other types in providing a significantly higher switching speed, at the expense of greater power consumption and therefore heating problems.

This combination of qualities means that ECL chips are used for logic circuits in systems where power is at a premium, such as large mainframes and superminis.

The most powerful ECL processor today is the one used in the Amdahl 5990 mainframe range, launched in May 1988. This has a power rating in excess of 30 mips.

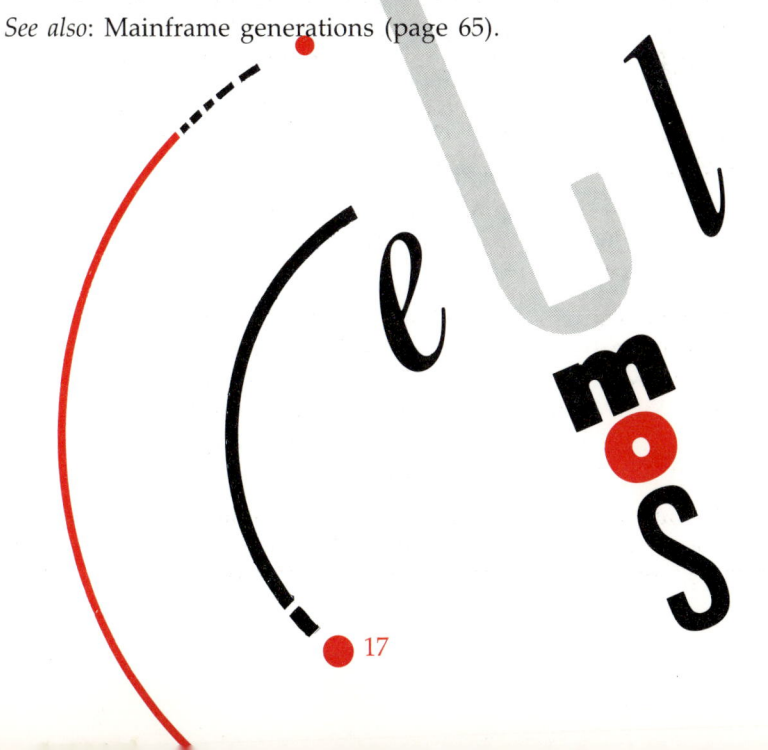

See also: Mainframe generations (page 65).

CYCLE TIME

The ultimate factor limiting the speed of operation of a computer system is the cycle time of its processor. Cycle times in modern systems range from about 10 nanoseconds for a vector processor or a large mainframe to about a microsecond for a low-cost, low performance PC. Processors thus have between one million and 100 million cycles per second in which to do work.

There is no direct relationship between the length of a processor cycle and that processor's throughput. Throughput is a function of the number of instructions executed. A typical mainframe or mini will have several hundred instructions in its instruction set, each of which takes between one and several cycles to execute.

Thus the number of instructions executed depends on the instruction mix, which in turn depends on the application (or application mix). As an example, the processor used in the Amdahl 5990 (the most powerful mainframe uniprocessor available today) operates at 100 million cycles a second, and produces throughput of a little over 30 million instructions per second (mips).

This ratio of around three cycles per instruction executed is fairly typical in large mainframes, which is why it is possible to compare mainframes using mips measurements with a reasonable degree of accuracy.

With other types of computer the ratio is different. The extreme is the reduced instruction set computer (Risc), where one of the design principles is to achieve one instruction execution per cycle.

For this reason Risc system mips are not comparable with non-Risc system mips: they suggest a much higher level of performance than is actually the case. (It is noteworthy that the only system for which IBM has ever quoted mips figures is the 6150 Risc range.)

The number of cycles taken to execute instructions is not the only variable in computer system performance. Maximum throughput will be achieved only if the processor has a task to execute and data to execute it with all the time.

Organising data flow through the system to achieve this is well nigh impossible; virtually all computers spend some of their machine cycles doing no work.

This is because the processor is the fastest part of the computer. Taking the IBM 3090 processor as an example, the cycle time is 15 nanoseconds (translating to about 65 million cycles a second). Main memory access time is only 80 nanoseconds, more than five times as long. Thus, when the processor needs to fetch data from main memory, it has to wait for four machine cycles or so before the data is available for work.

There are various ways round this problem. You can anticipate when you're going to need data, and fetch it from memory several cycles in advance. Or you can adopt stratagems which reduce the time to access memory for a large chunk of data by overlapping memory accesses. This technique, called memory interleaving, has been standard on mainframes since the early seventies and is now beginning to appear on PCs.

Here memory is divided into blocks. An access to block A is followed in the next machine cycle by an access to block B, and so on. The access to any one block still takes five machine cycles, but access to data spread over four blocks would take only eight cycles, rather than 20.

The simplest solution of all would be to make the memory the same speed as the processor. This would be prohibitively expensive on a mainframe or mini, but is a solution actually adopted on some PCs, where the processor cycle time is two or three times slower.

Most PC memories are of a technology type known as Dram (Dynamic random access memory). These have access times similar to those of mainframes, ranging down to about 80 nanoseconds.

Processor speeds for PCs are usually quoted in cycles per second, rather than the length of time of an individual cycle. A typical PC speed is 12 million cycles a second (12 MHz), which translates to a cycle time of around 83 nanoseconds. The fastest systems are rated at 25 MHz, or 40 nanoseconds.

For PCs of 12 MHz or less, Dram memories are fast enough to avoid the need for redundant memory cycles (known as wait states in PC terminology). The faster systems that have appeared over the past couple of years have brought mainframe and mini throughput problems down to the PC level.

One solution, adopted for example by Dell Computer, is to use Sram (static ram) memories. (Drams are dynamic because they lose electric charge over a period of time, and therefore constantly need to be refreshed. Srams don't.) Drams are cheaper than Srams, and use less power, but are slower. Using Srams thus allows an increase in memory speed at the expense of increasing the cost of the system.

A similar solution is to break the main memory into two levels, one operating at normal speed and the other operating at the speed of the processor. The faster one will need a more expensive type of technology, so will typically be very much smaller. Such a memory is known as a cache, or high-speed buffer.

The IBM 3090 processor has a cache size of 128Kb. This compares with the minimum main memory size of 32Mb, 250 times as large.

A cache is used to store the data and instructions most recently used. In the nature of computer operations, it turns out that a very high proportion of all instructions executed by a computer have been used recently. The same applies, to a lesser extent, with data.

Thus the majority, perhaps as much as 90%, of all memory accesses will only need to go to the cache. No processor cycles are wasted, so performance is substantially speeded up.

Once again, the effectiveness of a cache depends on the application. In some cases a dramatic improvement in performance is found, in others (especially those that handle large volumes of data) there is virtually none.

DATABASE

On early computer systems, users stored data in files, just as they had done in their previous manual systems. On many computers today, especially personal computers, this is still the case.

As computing developed, disadvantages gradually became apparent with file-based data storage. Many data items, such as customer and product details, were used by a number of different applications. These data items were therefore being stored several times, an inefficient and costly procedure.

Furthermore, adding new fields to files was difficult. It was easier to create a new file, taking only those data items you needed out of the old one and adding the additional data. This also led to duplication.

Any change to a data item stored on more than one file meant updating all relevant files, a problem that became more acute as real time transaction processing developed.

There was a need, therefore, for a new form of data organisation which would allow each data item to be stored once only, and to be accessible to every application program and every user who needed it. In this form of organisation, each data item is related to others in a structure which allows access to related data items efficiently.

This concept, which emerged in the early sixties, came to be known as a database. (The term is also used loosely to describe any related collection of data, irrespective of the degree of structure if any.) The database concept is a complex one which has no direct relationship to any manual filing method. As a result, a whole new sub-language has developed to describe various concepts used in database organisation.

Software products which provide facilities for creating and maintaining databases are known as database management systems (DBMS).

A user's description of the organisation and structure of a complete database is known as a schema. Users typically also specify the structure of the subset of the whole database used by specific applications programs. These structures are known as sub-schemas, or views.

Schemas and sub-schemas are written in a language provided with the DBMS and known as the data description language (DDL). Operations performed on a database by an application program are written in a language called a data manipulation language (DML).

All four of these concepts – schema, sub-schema, DDL and DML – were introduced in 1969 by a body called Codasyl (Conference of Data Systems Languages).

This body evolved a database standard, built around extensions to the Cobol programming language (which the same body had standardised earlier). Thus the DDL was defined as an extension to Cobol's data division, and the DML as an extension to the procedure division.

Codasyl recognised two types of database structure. The first, hierarchical, uses a tree-structure to organise data items, where each element is related to any number of elements below it in the structure, but to only one above it. The relationships are expressed by means of pointers. IBM's IMS is an example of a hierarchical database.

A networked database differs from the hierarchical type in that any given data element can be related to any number of other elements in both directions. Examples of successful networked databases are Cullinet's IDMS and Cincom's Total.

Networked and hierarchical database systems were widely used throughout the seventies and early eighties. Now however they are being superseded by a new type known as relational.

Here data is organised in the form of two-dimensional tables, consisting of columns and rows, a method of organisation which provides greater flexibility and does away with the need for pointers. Examples of relational databases are IBM's DB2, Oracle's Oracle and RTI's Ingres.

In 1988, Unisys became the first company to offer a fourth type of database, known as a semantic database. The main objective of this type of product is that it allows knowledge, rather than data, to be represented in the database.

This is done by capturing relationships between data items at the same time as the data itself. In contrast, in relational systems relations are specified by the application.

See also: Data dictionary (page 24), Distributed database (page 32), and Relational database (page 96).

DATA DICTIONARY

Once data independence – the separation of data from the programs that use it – began to be seen as desirable, and database management systems emerged to implement the concept, it quickly became apparent that there was a need for a new kind of utility.

It was necessary to store details of the attributes of data items, and to do so in a disciplined way which would prevent incomplete or inconsistent data definitions. Such a utility is known as a data dictionary.

A data dictionary contains the details about data items that were previously specified in applications programs – length of field, range of permitted values, numeric or alphabetic content and so on. It also contains details of the relationship of each item to other data items.

Since data dictionaries first appeared in the seventies, their role has evolved. In addition to data definitions, they can now contain screen formats, menu hierarchies and other standardised procedures relating to the operation of applications programs. To emphasise this greater comprehensiveness they are sometimes known as encyclopaedias.

Data dictionaries have also taken on a more important role. Initially they were merely a passive reference source, updated by the database administrator in the same way as a conventional file. Such dictionaries could be designed to run with a particular DBMS, or could be capable of use with any DBMS.

Today, many data dictionaries are active: that is, they are automatically kept up to date by the software that uses them, and are actively involved in the operation of an applications program. Active data dictionaries are always marketed as an integral part of a specific DBMS.

Data dictionaries are also playing a key role today in the systems development process, especially in environments where computer-aided systems engineering (Case) tools are in use.

Data dictionaries are proprietary products: there is no generally accepted standard. ANSI has been working on a standard called IRDS (Information Resource Dictionary System) since 1981, but this work has received little publicity and little support from the major vendors. ISO is also working on its own data dictionary standard.

See also: Database (page 21).

DATA PROTECTION

The problems of misuse of personal data held on computers began to concern people in the late sixties. At that time it began to be realised that computers offered an unprecedentedly powerful means of collecting together from different sources information about people. The potential existed for this information to be used in ways that would severely infringe individual privacy.

Examples of such potential infringements are the use of vehicle licensing records to track down people thought to owe tax; the use of data in police files to vet job applicants; and the use of bank records by credit-rating agencies.

These and many other examples were of concern in themselves. In addition, there were the problems of incorrect recording of information and the use of out-of-date information, both of which could have undesirable consequences for individuals.

Governments in advanced countries throughout the world began considering the possibility of specific legislation to prevent the abuse of personal information. In the UK the pressure started with the publication in 1968 of a pamphlet entitled "Privacy Under Attack" by the National Council for Civil Liberties.

Shortly afterwards the Government set up a committee to investigate the issue. Known as the Younger Committee after its chairman Kenneth Younger, it published its report in 1972.

This started a 12-year period of deliberation by Governments of both parties, punctuated by the publication of a White Paper in 1975, the Data Protection Committee report in 1978 and a second White Paper in 1982. The Data Protection Act was passed in 1984 and came fully into effect in 1987.

The long, drawn-out process meant, that although the UK was one of the first countries to consider data protection legislation, it was one of the last of the advanced nations to implement it, and eventually did so only under pressure from the Council of

Europe. Sweden was the first country to enact data protection legislation, in July 1973.

Under the Data Protection Act, computer users have become liable for compensation for personal damage resulting from loss of data or unauthorised access or disclosure of data.

Organisations holding personal data on computers must register with the Data Protection Registrar, declaring the uses to which the data will be put, and must not subsequently use it for any other purpose.

The Registrar is responsible for policing the Act and for bringing charges against anyone he believes is infringing it. Individuals who believe the law is being abused can complain to him, and they also gain under the Act the right of access to personal data held on them.

The provisions of the Act affect personal data held on computer systems only. Manual records are exempt.

DESIGN METHODOLOGIES

The need to approach systems development in a methodical fashion was first recognised in the sixties. It led quickly to the concept of modular programming, where large programs are broken down into small chunks, each of which can be written by a different programmer.

The idea has a number of advantages. First, simple tasks are easier to understand than more complicated ones. Second, each individual module can be tested and debugged separately; when the whole program is assembled and tested, any error found has to be due to a fault in the linkage, as each module is already known to be error-free.

Third, large programs can be written more quickly by a team than by a single individual.

Most important of all, the concept forced attention on the structure of a program. The way you split a program into modules and the way you linked the modules together became key issues. If these procedures were standardised, there was another important benefit: maintenance became easier, as listings were simpler to understand, and it also became independent of the original programmer.

So the structured programming concept was born. Promoted by gurus like Michael Jackson and Ed Yourdon, won widespread acceptance, so that today virtually every large program development centre adheres to one method or another.

Programming, however, is only part of the systems design process, so structured programming techniques solved only part of the problem. People gradually came to realise that the same structuring principles could profitably be applied to the whole systems design process.

This idea received a major boost in the UK in 1981, when the Central Computing and Telecommunications Agency (CCTA) decided to adopt a design methodology, and commissioned specialists Learmonth and Burchett to develop one for it.

The result, Structured Systems Analysis and Design Methodology (SSADM), has become a *de facto* standard for large Government computing projects, and has been used in developing over 600 Government systems.

SSADM defines a set of structural and procedural standards. As with structured programming, it allows users to break down development projects into a number of small components, which can be handled by different professionals in a controlled way.

There are a number of other design methodologies in use. Jackson and Yourdon are again to the fore, and so is James Martin, whose company James Martin Associates has, since 1981, been marketing a design methodology known as information engineering.

Information engineering differs from other methodologies in employing a top-down approach to systems design. You start with information strategy planning at the corporate level and move down through business area analysis before you get to the actual design and construction of systems. Thus there is a substantial initial effort to be made before any results can be achieved.

Put another way, information engineering concentrates on providing an understanding of the organisation as a whole by analysing the basic business processes and the information elements involved in them.

See also: Analyst workbench (page 5), Case (page 9).

DESKTOP PUBLISHING

A desktop publishing (DTP) system allows a user to produce printed output of a quality comparable to that found in books. It has facilities for mixing different type styles and sizes and adding in graphics all on the same page. In theory it ought to be possible also to print photographs, but the state of the art is not yet sufficiently advanced.

Desktop publishing has emerged as a computing application only within the past three to four years. This is because it requires a combination of fast processing speed, high-resolution screen and high-resolution printer at single-user system prices (£5,000 to £10,000), and the necessary technology has only recently been developed.

The product which triggered the development of desktop publishing was the Apple Macintosh, launched in 1984. The Mac packaged together a high-resolution screen with a graphics-based user-friendly interface at a realistic price.

It was followed by the Apple Laserwriter printer a year later. That completed the hardware infrastructure: all that was then necessary was the software. The first packages appeared in late 1985.

For a while, Apple had the market to itself (the company is still today the market leader). In late 1986, packages started to appear for the IBM PC, and it was then that desktop publishing started to demand serious attention from large corporate users. Since then, the 32-bit PC has arrived, with internal processing speeds of up to 25 MHz, and this level of power looks set to make desktop publishing a routine business application over the next few years.

Butler Cox estimates that some 30% of European businesses have desktop publishing systems installed today. They are projecting a rapid rise to 90% by 1990, by which time the market will be worth over $1 billion.

There are three elements in a desktop publishing system. First, a PC, today almost universally a Mac, an IBM PC or compatible, though systems are starting to appear for the PS/2 which looks set to become the standard hardware base.

Second, a software package. There are more than 30 packages on the UK market today. Some are extensions of familiar word processing packages with page make-up facilities added; others have been designed from scratch. Aldus Corp's Page Maker is the market leader, with Xerox's Ventura Publisher at number two.

Third, a printer. Laser printers are the most common, with Apple's Laserwriter and Hewlett-Packard's Laserjet leading the market. Typically printers provide a resolution of 300 dots to the inch, and are rated theoretically at around eight pages per minute, though these speeds are rarely obtained in practice.

Prices range from around £1,500 upwards. Dot matrix printers provide a cheaper alternative: devices using matrices of up to 24 characters are available for under £1,000.

DISTRIBUTED DATABASE

With the development of networks of computers, each with its own information store, there is emerging a need for software which allows data retrieval from any physical location in the network without the user needing to know where the data is stored.

Taken to its logical extreme, users should be able to access various different data items needed by an application in different places, and assemble them into a whole at their own terminals. A piece of software which provides these facilities is known as a distributed database management system (DDBMS).

A DDBMS offers two major potential advantages. First, resilience: in the event of hardware or software failure at the central location, or a failure of communications between the centre and a remote site, most users will still be able to access most data.

Second, cost saving: if data storage is so organised that each part of the database is stored at the location which uses it most, then communications traffic is minimised.

The DDBMS is still an emerging concept, with development running about 12 years behind the development of relational database systems. As with the latter, 12 rules describing the ideal characteristics of a DDBMS have been formulated, though this time the expert is not Edgar Codd but his business partner, Chris Date.

These rules include such provisions as that a DDBMS should be hardware, operating system and network independent, and that you should be able to add new sites without having to close the system down temporarily.

Systems which conform more or less to Date's ideal started to appear in the early eighties; one of the first was D-Net from Applied Data Research, launched in 1983.

More recently, leading RDBMS suppliers RTI and Oracle have

released distributed versions of their established packages, known as Ingres-Star and SQL-Star respectively.

IBM has announced limited distributed capabilities for its flagship relational system, DB2, for delivery in late 1989. The company has promised it will extend these facilities in time, in line with customer demand.

See also: Database (page 21).

EDI

EDI (electronic data interchange) is a term which emerged in the mid-eighties, though the idea had been discussed for much longer. The impetus for action in the UK came with the deregulation of British Telecom and the arrival of Vans (value-added network services).

EDI is analogous with EFT (electronic funds transfer), except that the data interchanged relates to a business transaction (typically an order or an invoice) rather than a financial transaction.

Data transfer is more complicated than funds transfer, as can be appreciated by comparing invoices from half a dozen randomly chosen companies with cheques from half a dozen banks. Every company has its own document formats; every industry has its own specialised ordering and invoicing practices.

Setting up an EDI service, therefore, involves devising a standard format for each type of transaction that suits all participants. Work on developing a standard that could be used as a basis for all such services started as early as 1971, and was initiated by a UK organisation, Sitpro (Simplification of International Trade Procedures Board).

The United Nations later became involved, and in 1980 published Guidelines for Trade Data Interchange (GTDI). These guidelines were followed in all the early EDI services in the UK.

With the experience gained in pioneer services in both Europe and the US, a new set of syntax rules has been evolved by the International Standards Organisation. These are known as Edifact (EDI For Administration, Commerce and Transport).

Both GTDI and more recently Edifact have been used to develop standard formats for various transaction types for a specific industry sector.

Different vendors, however, have been developing different standards for the same industry. Standardisation at industry level is now one of the most pressing EDI concerns.

Various things are being done to tackle the problem. Leading suppliers banded together in 1987 to form Idea (International Data Exchange Association), whose major aim is to promote standardisation. An Esprit-funded project started in 1988 with the objective of coordinating the different projects being run in different EEC member states.

The transaction formats are the heart of an EDI service. In addition, the vendor has to provide a network to enable the participants to communicate with each other, plus facilities for each participant to translate messages into and out of the standardised format. This process is complicated by the fact that the participants are naturally going to have a wide range of different computers.

Typically, an EDI service user will carry out the necessary protocol and format conversion on its own computer. The output, transaction data in the required standardised format, is transmitted into the EDI network, and stored temporarily in a mailbox on the EDI central computer until the recipient is ready to process it. The data is then translated by the destination company into the form required by its computer prior to processing.

The potential advantages of EDI are considerable: the elimination of data entry at the recipient's end, which not only saves time and money in itself but also removes a major source of error; savings in paper and postage bills; reduction in stock inventories; and improvements to cashflow.

These benefits have attracted many companies into the EDI service market over the past three or four years. IBM, International Network Services (a joint ICL/Geisco venture) and Istel are three of the most prominent UK EDI vendors. Major application areas are the automobile, chemical, construction electronics and tourism industries.

See also: Vans (page 117).

ESPRIT

Esprit (European Strategic Programme for Research in Information Technology) is an EEC initiative designed to enable the European IT industry to compete effectively with the American and Japanese competition during the 1990s.

It is providing funds for R&D in three main areas: microelectronics; software technology; and applications (with emphasis on office automation and computer-integrated manufacturing [Cim]).

Each project must involve at least two partners, each from a different EEC member country. In practice, there are typically about five organisations involved per project, and some of the larger ones have more than 10 partners.

Esprit started in 1983 with a pilot programme involving funding of 11.5 million ECUs (£7.2 million) and around 30 projects. The main programme, with funding of 750 million ECUs (£465 million), started the following year, and is just coming to fruition now.

Each project is funded 50:50 by the EEC and the participating organisations. The total value of investment in Esprit to date is therefore a little under £1 billion.

To capitalise on the results of the research so far, the EEC has now decided to fund a second phase programme, known as Esprit 2. Its scope is similar to that of the first phase, but is more market-oriented.

A substantially larger budget, 1,600 million ECUs (£1.1 billion) has been allocated by the EEC to cover the cost of Esprit 2 over five years.

Since Esprit was originally mooted, two other pan-European research programmes have been devised. The first is Race (Research in Advanced Communications in Europe). Another EEC initiative which is similar in size of funding to Esprit 1, Race has two objectives.

The first is the development of a reference model for an integrated broadband communications system, to allow the transmission of large volumes of information of all kinds at high speed. The second is to work out the economic and technical feasibility of the infrastructure of products and services needed to support such a system.

As with Esprit, Race started off with a small pilot programme involving 30 projects. That was in 1986; the main phase received budget approval in early 1988.

The other major European research programme is Eureka. This was initiated by the French Government in 1985 in response to the American Strategic Defense Initiative ("Star Wars"), and is intended to help Europe develop the enabling technologies for space research.

Unlike Esprit and Race, Eureka is not confined to EEC member countries, and a total of 18 nations are participating. Budget allocations were initially a matter for each country individually, though the EEC has now taken over this responsibility as far as its members are concerned.

See also: Fifth generation (page 43).

ETHERNET

Ethernet is a type of local area network (Lan). It was originally developed by Xerox, and has since been made the subject of a formal standard by both the European Computer Manufacturers' Association (Ecma) and the Institute of Electrical and Electronics Engineers (IEEE).

Ethernet implements the bottom two layers of ISO's seven-layer model, the layers which define the physical hardware and signalling properties. It uses CSMA/CD (carrier sense multiple access/collision detection) baseband signalling along coaxial cables, and data is transmitted in variable length packets at a speed of 10 Mbits a second.

Historically, Ethernet was developed by Xerox at its Palo Alto Research Centre (the term is still a Xerox trademark). The objective was to link word processors into prototype office automation networks – at the time, in 1976, personal computers as we know them today did not exist.

When the need arose for local area networks to connect PCs, Xerox spotted a market opportunity, and published the Ethernet specification in 1980.

Over 250 companies applied for licences within two years, among them industry giants DEC and Intel which quickly decided to commit to Ethernet as a standard communications medium.

Their backing proved crucial in persuading two standards-making bodies, Ecma in Europe and IEEE in the US, to develop standards based on Ethernet.

In the event, the three versions were marginally different, but the variations have been eliminated since.

See also: Lan (page 58).

EXPERT SYSTEM

An expert system is a software package which uses artificial intelligence techniques to formulate value judgments in answer to qualitative questions, basing those judgments on a body of information supplied by specialists.

For example, a medical expert system might ask for details of a patient's symptoms, and then offer an opinion as to what might be wrong. The opinion would be based on information supplied by doctors, and would be arrived at by applying mathematically based probability theory.

Some systems will give you a list of different possible answers, indicating the degree of probability for each. Others will, if required, explain their decision.

Expert systems have a history dating back to the late sixties, but it is only in the last few years that they have become widespread. This has come about because of the development of expert systems packages for PCs, particularly the IBM PC.

These packages are of two types. You can buy a ready-to-run system, complete with "knowledge base" covering a specific subject. An example is a system which advises users on what they need to do to comply with the Data Protection Act.

Alternatively, you can buy a shell, which contains all the facilities you need to develop your own tailor-made system. Companies selling shells for the IBM PC include Expertech, Expert Systems International and Helix Expert Systems.

Expert system shells enable you to capture the expertise of an expert in, theoretically at least, any subject, and retain it for use when the expert is unavailable.

Use of an expert system can therefore speed up the decision-making processes even of other experts, and can also help novices become productive much more quickly.

Expert systems have limitations, and should not be thought of as substitutes for human judgment. They have been successful only when the sphere of expertise has been both narrow and tightly defined. The major application areas are finance, engineering, travel and medicine. They are also extensively used within the computer industry itself.

See also: Artificial intelligence (page 7).

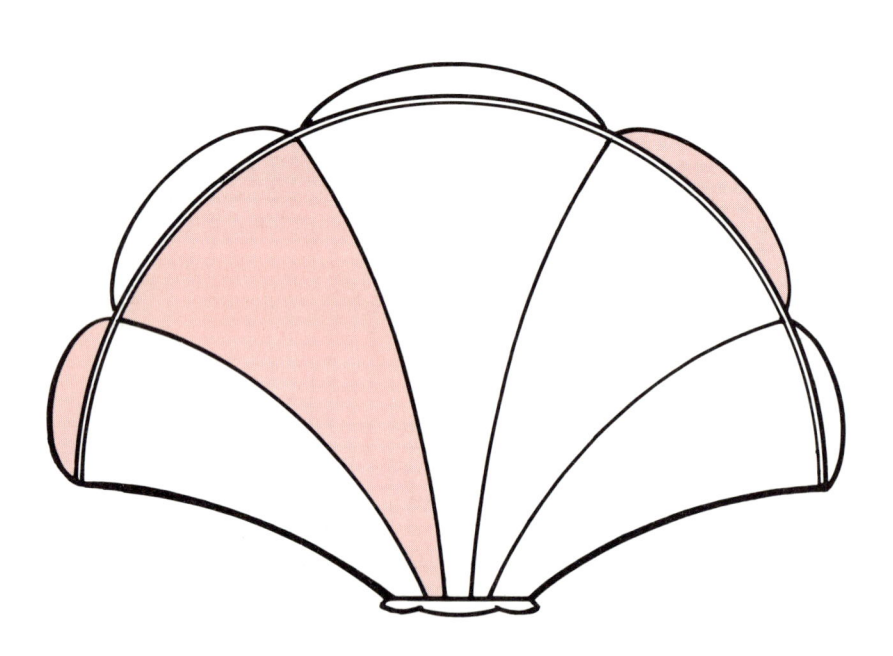

FAULT TOLERANCE

As computers have become more essential to a company's business, so avoiding breakdowns has become more critical. The change from batch to online transaction processing accentuated the trend; a computer failure for any length of time could mean a substantial loss of business, especially in the financial world.

Techniques for minimising the impact of breakdowns led to the development of the multiprocessor system, particularly by Burroughs and Univac (the two halves of what is now Unisys), to the adoption of standby generators, and to the development of uninterruptible power supplies.

A small start-up company in California took a different course, sensing that the need for highly reliable operation created a market for a new type of computer system. That company was Tandem Computers, which was formed in 1974 and brought its first Nonstop system to the market two years later.

The Nonstop architecture provides what is essentially a software solution to the problem of ensuring reliability. It was built round a proprietary operating system called TOS which was developed specifically for transaction processing. TOS provided database protection, and also protected against loss of transactions.

Tandem's software solution was backed up by appropriate precautions against hardware failure. Every system component that could be duplicated was duplicated. There was a minimum of two processors, with a separate copy of the operating system in each one, and duplicated inter-processor buses.

"Nonstop" was Tandem's trade name for its product range. "Failsafe" was the name applied to this generic class of systems until around 1982, when the current term "fault tolerant" came into use.

This is not merely a semantic change. "Failsafe" implies that in the event of any system failure there will be no adverse consequences. Tandem systems could be set up to run failsafe, but this involved a fair amount of user programming which few users felt it necessary to undertake.

"Fault tolerant" implies merely that any fault will result in a tolerable state of affairs. This is both less complex and less expensive than completely failsafe operation. It also reflects what most users want: that faults should be kept to a minimum; that they cause minimum disruption when they do occur; and that they take minimum effort to recover from.

The fault-tolerant system market developed from the moment Tandem first started deliveries. After four years of exceptional growth, the company's first rival, Stratus, appeared.

Stratus took a different, more hardware-based approach to the problem (emphasising that fault tolerance is an approach rather than a particular technique or architecture). In the Stratus system, each chip on the processor was duplicated, so that if one fails the other can take over. This contrasts with the duplication at the processor level adopted by Tandem.

Stratus has since been joined by a number of other companies, among them the only British supplier, Information Technology Ltd (ITL).

The mainframe manufacturers have also become interested. Honeywell Bull offers fault-tolerant versions of the two processor models in its DPS 88 and DPS 90 ranges. NCR's 9800 range has fault-tolerant features, though there is as yet little software to take advantage of it. IBM has taken out a licence to sell Stratus products under its own name as the System 88.

Other manufacturers offer various aspects of fault tolerance to cater for specific system vulnerabilities that users could be worried about. Disc mirroring – the technique of writing data to two separate disc systems simultaneously – is becoming an increasingly common option, reflecting the fact that disc hardware is the most vulnerable part of most computer systems.

FIFTH GENERATION

The fifth generation is a concept introduced by the Japanese in the late seventies to describe a new type of computer, expected to replace existing computers during the next decade.

The fifth generation differs from its four predecessors in its architecture, which will be designed for parallel processing.

Until now all data processing computers have been sequential processors, performing one operation on one piece of data at a time.

This limits machine performance. It has not so far been a significant constraint except in scientific computing, but is expected to affect large-scale data processing users over the next five to 10 years.

Current machine architecture also imposes constraints on programming languages, which of necessity must mirror the machine's characteristics. In essence, this means that each language instruction relates to a procedure to be followed by a computer, rather than to a requirement for action by a human being.

"Non-procedural" languages have been developed: examples are Lisp and Prolog. However, these languages tend to perform poorly on present-day computers.

The importance of non-procedural languages is that they allow systems to be built much more easily and reliably. Ease of use is another key characteristic of the fifth generation, and much effort is being devoted to the design of appropriate user interfaces.

As well as better performance and greater ease of use, the fifth generation will naturally incorporate all predicted advances in technology.

One consequence of this is that they will have memories several orders of magnitude larger than today's computers, a key requirement for natural language processing.

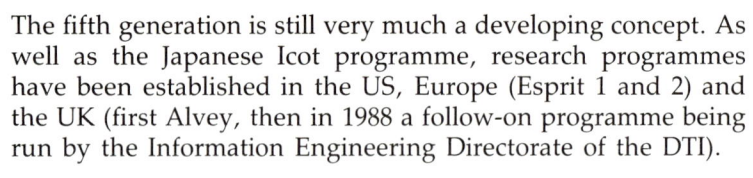

The fifth generation is still very much a developing concept. As well as the Japanese Icot programme, research programmes have been established in the US, Europe (Esprit 1 and 2) and the UK (first Alvey, then in 1988 a follow-on programme being run by the Information Engineering Directorate of the DTI).

See also: Esprit (page 36).

FILE SERVER

The term "file server" is one that entered computing vocabulary with the arrival of the local area network (Lan).

A server is a shared resource on a network; a device which provides a service to all the terminals and workstations on it. A file server thus provides a centralised filing service and typically consists of a Winchester disc, a processor and file management software.

A file server is used for two reasons. First, it is more economic to have one large fixed disc centrally than many small discs attached to the individual workstations. Second, most networks need a common pool of corporate information to be available to most or all of the network users.

Networks may also have other types of server. A print server, for example, can provide high-speed, high-quality centralised printing more economically than use of multiple matrix and daisy wheel printers.

A communications server can similarly provide centralised access to other corporate networks and to public services such as Prestel and Telecom Gold.

As with many computing terms, this one was no sooner coined than its meaning began to be extended. One hears, for example, of mainframes being described as file servers to the networks they support, because the main service they provide to the terminal users is access to the corporate database.

See also: Lan (page 58).

FOURTH GENERATION LANGUAGE

Fourth generation language is one of the multitude of computing terms which has no generally agreed meaning. "Buyer beware" is the order of the day: don't allow yourself to be seduced by technospeak.

The concept was invented to symbolise the advances made in programming since the first third generation languages appeared in the fifties. But whereas these languages – Cobol and Fortran are the most widely used – were clearly distinguished from their predecessors, the second generation assembler languages, there is no such sharp dividing line between the third and fourth generations.

The advances made since the introduction of Fortran and Cobol can be classified under three heads. First, programming productivity has increased in terms of either a reduction in coding time or a reduction in overall system development time.

Second, systems development has moved away from the specialist programmer towards the end-user in a variety of ways.

Third, programming can be conducted at a higher level: that is, the number of source program statements required to achieve a given degree of functionality has declined.

The terms "fourth generation language" and "fourth generation development tool" are applied to any product which embodies any of these advances. There are three distinct types of product which meet this requirement.

First, program generators (sometimes called applications generators). These are products which in various ways reduce the mental effort required to produce a given amount of code. Some are intended to improve the productivity of professional programmers, others are designed to make it possible for end-users to write their own programs.

Examples are the Unisys products Linc and Mapper for mainframes, and the much-publicised The Last One for micros.

Second, there are special-purpose packages which are supplied with systems development tools. Most database management systems today fall into this category, even packages for personal computers such as Ashton-Tate's dBase family. Spreadsheet systems fall under this heading too.

Third, there are conventional third generation programming languages which, in the view of their advocates, are substantially more advanced than the others in one of the respects mentioned.

Examples are RPG, which can readily be used by non-programmers to develop reports, and APL, which has a very high level of functionality per source program statement.

No reliable measure exists to show how much any of these fourth generation systems increases productivity compared with its third generation predecessors.

Marketing claims put the improvement at as much as 10:1, but detailed academic research shows that this is unfounded. The true figure, taking the whole system development cycle into account, is probably not more than 3:1.

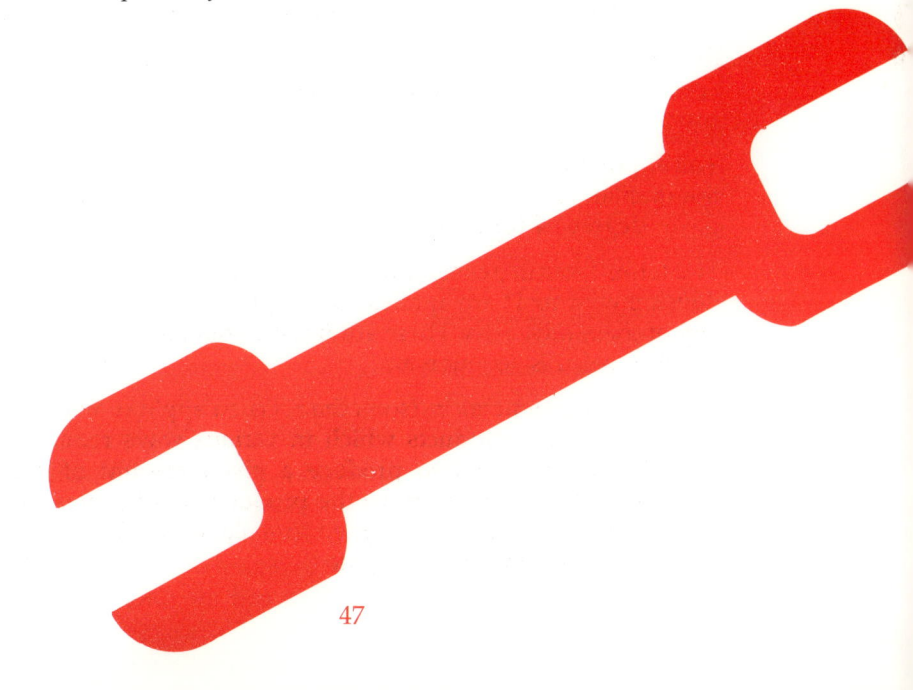

FUNCTION POINT

The applications backlog and the skills shortage are two interrelated problems that bedevil just about every computer installation. Managing both would be much easier if we had some kind of reasonably accurate measure of software productivity.

For many years most attempts at measuring productivity have centred on counting lines of code, and then relating the answer to either time or cost. This has proved unsatisfactory for a variety of reasons, all of which stem from the fact that lines of code are not an end-product: it is the working system that the user wants.

One of the most serious drawbacks of line of code counts is that they cannot be used to compare programs written in different languages, still less programs written in different levels of language.

An assembler language program written to perform a given task will have many more lines of code than, say, a Cobol program written to perform the same task, which will in turn have more lines than a fourth generation language program.

If therefore you measure lines of code produced against time or cost, you will normally find that programmers are most "productive" in using assembler. They may certainly produce more lines of code per unit of time, but overall system development is usually slower and subsequent maintenance costs are invariably very much higher.

Various attempts have been made to overcome this problem. One of the most promising was advanced by an IBM researcher, AJ Albrecht, in 1979, using a concept known as function points.

Albrecht was essentially attempting to measure software productivity according to the functionality of the program produced, rather than its length. Function point calculations therefore take account of what the program does, measured in terms of inputs, outputs, master files and interfaces.

A function point itself is an abstract concept, not related to any identifiable quality of a program. Its value can be demonstrated by expressing the number of source statements required to code one in each of several languages.

Software productivity expert Capers Jones has published a table which shows that it takes 320 assembler language statements to code one function point. You'd need 106 statements in both Cobol and Fortran, 71 in Ada, 64 in Basic, 16 in a typical query language and a mere six in one of the spreadsheet languages.

Jones notes that the margin of error in his table is fairly high, and this brings us on to the technique's drawbacks. First, there is a degree of uncertainty in how to count inputs, outputs and other program elements (just as arguments rage over what constitutes a line of code).

Second, there is an element of subjectivity involved in taking account of variables not allowed for in the basic function point calculations. The degree of computational complexity is an example: this affects the results to such a degree that function points have been much more effective with data processing programs than with scientific or real time programs (that is, where data complexity is high and computational complexity low rather than vice versa).

For all that, function point calculations have produced useful results in academic circles, as well as promoting greater understanding of the problems of measuring software productivity.

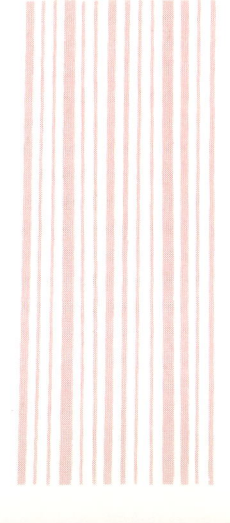

GALLIUM ARSENIDE

The basic building block used to construct virtually every computer that has appeared since the early seventies is the silicon chip. It is used to build both processor logic and memory units (Ram and Rom).

There are several different types of silicon chip, falling into two major classes, bipolar and Mos, and several sub-classes. They provide different trade-offs between key variables, such as switching speed, power consumption and price. Silicon is used in all of them because of its particular combination of chemical properties and because it is abundant and therefore cheap.

There is only one alternative semiconducting material to silicon that is at all commonly used in the manufacture of integrated circuits, and that is gallium arsenide (GaAs). It has two important qualities that have prompted its use in certain types of application.

First, gallium arsenide provides slightly faster switching speeds than silicon – between three and 10 times, depending on the implementation.

The second advantage that GaAs has over silicon is its much greater ability to withstand radiation. It can tolerate exposure to microwave transmissions and laser beams, and can operate at temperatures some 200° higher than silicon.

This combination of qualities makes gallium arsenide suitable for applications in military environments, in satellites and in optical devices. These applications explain why UK Government-backed research into the technology has until 1987 taken place only within the Ministry of Defence.

In January 1987, however, the Department of Trade and Industry announced it was allocating £25 million for gallium arsenide research. This reflects recognition of the material's potential in non-military applications, such as in car engines and in high- speed computer systems.

Leading supercomputer manufacturer Cray Research has been developing a gallium arsenide system to be known as the Cray-3. This is now expected to be launched in late 1989, and is said to be four times as powerful as the company's current top model, the Y-MP.

Gallium arsenide will not replace silicon in computers generally for one simple reason – gallium is a much rarer element and is therefore substantially more expensive. Market research firm Dataquest says GaAs chips cost 10 to 15 times as much as their silicon alternative.

IPSE

Integrated project support environment (Ipse) is the name given to an integrated set of systems development tools which cover the specification, design, programming, building and testing of computer systems. The term is now usually used to mean a set of tools that is independent of the programming language used.

The Ipse concept evolved from a feeling of concern that software productivity has improved at a much slower rate than hardware productivity, thus upsetting their economic ratio.

This feeling particularly concerned planners in the US Department of Defense who formulated the specification for Ada, their new standardised real time programming language.

The prime objective behind Ada was the need to reduce program maintenance costs. When producing the Ada specification, the Department recognised that the design, implementation and testing of large programs was very error-prone because programmers have to master too many details at once.

The solution was Ada, a language which would easily permit a programming development to be broken down into many small tasks. An essential part of Ada was the support environment, known as Apse (Ada programming support environment).

Once the Apse concept was publicised, it was recognised quickly that the idea was valid for all programming languages, not just Ada. Various bodies have since begun to develop Ipses, and it has now become an integral part of fifth generation thinking.

The first Ipses started to appear in the early eighties, though there are still only a handful on the market. One of the most successful so far is Philips Maestro, which is used by the Inland Revenue and British Gas. Other companies in the market include BIS (BIS/lpse), GEC Software (Genos), Imperial Software Technology (Istar) and SD-Scicon (Perspective).

These are all proprietary products. Two other Ipses have been developed with public funding. They are PCTE and Cais.

PCTE (Portable Common Tool Environment) came out of an Esprit project, and all current Esprit developments must themselves use PCTE. Cais (Common Apse Interface Set) is a parallel American development that is supported by the US Department of Defense.

See also: Case (page 9).

ISDN

The convergence of the traditionally separate areas of voice and data communications has been widely forecast. It hasn't happened yet, but considerable progress has been made. The same public networks are used for both types of traffic, and some of the supporting products – exchanges and multi-function workstations – have begun to appear.

In most organisations still, however, voice and data networks are run separately and are totally unconnected. It is desirable to integrate them – this would avoid duplication of products and of cabling as well as reducing administrative overheads.

These potential advantages are the motivating force behind the development of ISDN (Integrated Services Digital Network). ISDN will be an internationally standardised network like the phone system, but differing from it in that both voice and data transmissions can be sent down the same digital line.

The ISDN standards are being formulated by CCITT, the representative body of the world's national postal and telephone authorities. The standards, which are technically described as "recommendations", are referred to by code numbers prefixed by the letter I. An example is I.420, which describes a basic 144Kbps ISDN interface.

Several countries are running pilot trials of ISDN services, including France, Japan, the US and West Germany. The UK was one of the pioneers: British Telecom's pilot ISDN service, known as IDA (Integrated Digital Access), started in June 1985.

IDA, like Kilostream and Megastream, uses the trunk network and System X digital exchanges. The difference is in the lines connecting the exchanges to the customer.

Two types are offered. The single-line version gives the user two parallel digital paths, one operating at 64Kbps for both voice and data transmission, the other operating at 8Kbps for data only. The multiline version provides 30 digital paths each operating at 64Kbps; all can be used for either voice and data. Both versions use separate paths for signalling information.

A problem has arisen with the trial services like IDA: because the CCITT has not completed the standards-making process, each carrier has had to develop its own solutions to fill the gaps. These solutions vary from country to country and so the various trials are incompatible with each other, a development which is worrying both the CCITT and the EEC.

Since single-line IDA was launched, for example, it has become incompatible with the CCITT single-line ISDN in two major respects. First, the CCITT standard specifies two 64Kbps paths instead of one 64Kbps and one 8Kbps path, plus a 16Kbps signalling path in place of an 8Kbps signalling path, yielding a total line transmission speed of 144Kbps compared with IDA's 80Kbps. (This CCITT recommendation is often abbreviated to 2B+D.) Second, CCITT has specified the I.420 interface for connecting terminals to the line. IDA requires use of the X.21 interface.

The position is worse with multiline ISDN, as CCITT has yet to define what will be required apart from the basic capacity of 30 64Kbps paths plus two 64Kbps signalling paths (for a total line transmission speed of 2Mbps). Accordingly, BT has had to invent its own "standards" to get the pilot service running at all.

This uncertainty, coupled with the tariff structure applied by BT, has meant that few companies have yet started experimenting with single-line IDA, and virtually none with the multiline version.

British Telecom has committed itself to adhere to CCITT standards once they appear (it has already uprated single-line IDA to the 2B+D specification). It has further promised to provide upwards compatibility from any different procedures it has adopted in the interim.

These promises have been insufficient to allay its customers' worries. It now seems likely that ISDN integrated voice and data communications will not be widely adopted until well into the next decade.

ISO

Many different organisations make standards which affect the life of computer professionals. Some of them are specialist technical organisations, such as Ecma (European Computer Manufacturers' Association) and IEEE (Institute of Electrical and Electronic Engineers); others are national bodies, such as BSI (British Standards Institution) and ANSI (American National Standards Institute).

More important than any of these is ISO (International Standards Organisation). ISO's authority is multinational and worldwide, and spans all areas of manufactured goods. Its activities are particularly valuable in the area of telecomms, where widely accepted international standards are a must if the principles of open systems interconnection (OSI) are to be realised.

ISO operates through a series of technical committees, one for each category of product. The committee devoted to information processing is known as TC97, and has one of the largest subject areas of all ISO technical committees.

TC97 is responsible for strategic work, such as reviewing the acceptance of existing standards, supervising the progress of proposed new standards and deciding when a standard is needed. The work of formulating standards is delegated to sub-committees, of which TC97 has two dozen. Sometimes the sub-committees themselves feel their brief is too wide and delegate further to working groups.

In most cases the ISO does not start from scratch. Work done in the BSI or Ecma or CCITT acts as a starting point, and in these cases some of the people who worked on the lesser bodies' standards are appointed to the appropriate TC97 sub-committee (or working group). This ensures a familiarisation with the intricacies of the problem and helps to minimise differences between, say, Ecma standards and ISO standards.

The procedure for ratifying an ISO standard is a lengthy one – it usually takes several years. There are three distinct stages.

First, the sub-committee produces a draft proposal. This document is effectively the best compromise between the specialists in whatever the chosen field (programming languages, office automation, telecomms, etc). It is referred to by a number prefixed by the letters DP.

Time is allowed for discussion and for interested parties to make comments or objections before the next stage, which is review by the technical committee. This committee is comprised of specialists in all areas of information processing, and considers the draft proposal in the light of the broader needs of the whole IT world.

The result of this work is a draft international standard, referred to by the same reference number but this time prefixed by the letters DIS.

There is then a similar pause for reflection and comment before review by ISO itself, considering the needs of the whole world rather than just the IT part of it. In practice, this procedure rarely makes any substantial change, but it is not until it is completed that the international standard can truly be said to exist. The outcome is a document with the same reference number prefixed by the letters IS.

The procedure is necessarily lengthy to ensure that the needs of all interest groups are accommodated, so that the resulting standard will have a wide measure of acceptance. The delay can be irksome, however, when standards are urgently needed, which is why bodies like Ecma with a one-stage ratification process are able to perform valuable preparatory groundwork, and many of their standards are widely quoted.

ISO standards in their final form are available from the BSI.

LAN

A local area network (Lan) is an interconnected group of personal computers or workstations.

Typically, each station is capable of standalone operation, but shares with other stations on the network expensive facilities such as mass disc storage, fast laser printing and communications with external systems.

The grouping is geographically circumscribed within a small area, with an upper maximum cable length of a kilometre or two. Usually, this means a single building, or perhaps two or three floors within a building.

Functionally a Lan is a means of distributing computer power among a large number of users working in the same place.

The same objective can be reached by scattering standalone systems, with multi-user micros, and with conventional networks linking intelligent terminals to a mainframe or minicomputer.

Compared with multiple standalone systems, Lans provide economies of scale in both peripherals and communications lines and equipment. They also offer the benefits of standardisation and make for easier management control.

Compared with the other two alternatives, Lans sit in the middle. Multiuser micros are generally cheaper, but serve a smaller number of users, and each user is more heavily dependent on the central processor. Purpose-built terminal networks are more expensive, but offer more central processor power and are not confined to a small local area.

There has been much discussion about the best way to configure a local area network, and to organise the communications between the different network elements. No universal solution has emerged from these arguments.

The Ethernet system has won wide acceptance, but token ring Lans such as the one sold by IBM operate on totally different principles. It seems likely that there will always be several different types; the choice between them will depend on the application and the pattern of usage.

See also: Ethernet (page 38), File server (page 45), and Token ring (page 113).

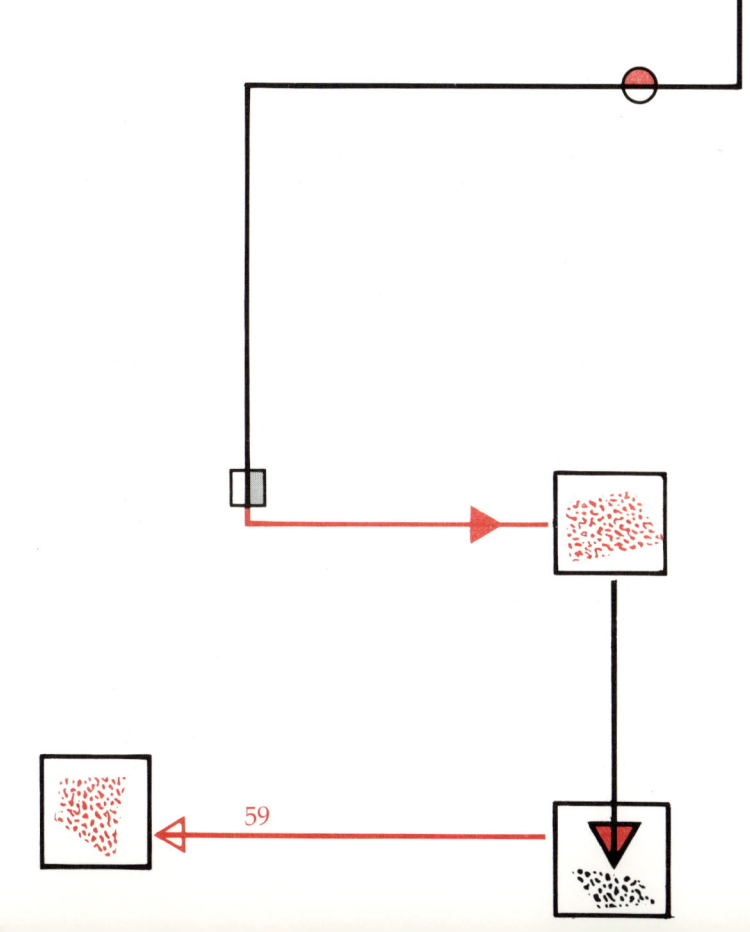

LU 6.2

LU 6.2 (Logical Unit 6.2) is a protocol defined by IBM as part of its Systems Network Architecture (SNA). It defines the rules governing how two programmable devices communicate with each other within an SNA network.

LU 6.2 is one of several different logical unit protocols. Each one defines an interface between "end-users" (either an application program or a terminal operator) and the network. The different protocols are needed for the different types of logical device an end-user may work through.

Logical units specify the procedural rules under which communication between two end-users proceeds. Examples of procedures specified are the formatting of data, the amount of data sent by one user before the other replies, and the action to be taken if an error occurs.

These logical rules operate irrespective of the physical devices (terminals, printers) used in communication. There is a separate set of physical unit (PU) protocols, which governs the establishment and maintenance of communication between physical units, or strictly speaking between nodes of a network. Every SNA node must contain one physical unit, but can contain one or more logical units.

LU 6.2 is the most important of the logical unit protocols, and the one readers are most likely to come across. This is because it is very different from the other LU protocols: it considers the logical units involved in communication as equals. Either logical unit can initiate a conversation with the other.

This type of communication is known as peer-to-peer. It contrasts with a master-slave arrangement, whereby communications are controlled by a central host, and all links between any two nodes on the network have to be routed through that host.

SNA was initially developed in the seventies, when nearly all computer networks consisted of a mainframe plus terminals. A master-slave topology was therefore the natural one to adopt.

Since then, though, the trend towards distributed processing and departmental computing has made peer-to-peer communications more attractive, as you avoid the bottleneck caused by the need to reroute all communications through the host. LU 6.2 is the vehicle IBM is using as the base for peer-to-peer communications, hence its importance.

LU 6.2 is implemented using a software product called Advanced Program-to-Program Communications (APPC). For this reason, you will often find LU 6.2 and APPC treated as synonyms.

Until mid-1987, LU 6.2 communications were possible only between applications using the CICS teleprocessing monitor. At that time IBM issued a new release of VTAM (effectively IBM's operating system for SNA networks), which also supports LU 6.2. This has greatly increased its importance, as virtually all IBM wide area networks use VTAM, and VTAM interfaces to all IBM's major software utilities.

Since then, IBM has further underlined the strategic significance of LU 6.2 by nominating APPC as the component within Systems Application Architecture (SAA) for peer-to-peer communications.

See also: SNA (page 102).

MAINFRAME, MINI, MICRO

Computer systems are generally divided into three main classes: mainframes, minis and micros. Subdivisions of these classes are also found, such as supercomputers, superminis and personal computers. These terms have some meaning inasmuch as they reflect historical evolution, but there are no precise definitions or dividing lines between the classes.

The first computers were, in today's nomenclature, supercomputers. Eniac, Edsac and their contemporaries in the 1940s were designed to perform complex scientific calculations that could not be handled by any other machine of the time. The Crays of today are their logical successors.

Although the computer was invented (as its name implies) for computational problems, it was soon realised that it could be applied to data processing problems – the processing of administrative tasks such as invoicing, payroll and stock control. These tasks are characterised by a minimum of computation (and what there is trivial) and a great deal of data manipulation (input and output work).

Probably the first company to realise this, and certainly the first to take action, was J Lyons & Co, the corner tea-shop chain. Lyons set to work to build a computer that was based on Edsac, but had the improved I/O facilities necessary for commercial DP.

The project started in 1947, and the result, Leo I, produced its first live results in 1954. Leo I was the first system we would today class as a mainframe.

Lyons' vision was soon shared by others, and the production of computers for sale began in the early fifties. The vast majority of computer sales were (and are to this day) for data processing applications, with scientific sales remaining a small-volume activity.

Leo I and its contemporaries were simply called "computers": the term "mainframe" did not come into general use till the

1960s. It was needed then to differentiate between mainframes and the newly arrived minicomputer.

The minicomputer was originally vastly different from the mainframe. The applications were different – process control, and what we would now regard as programmable calculator tasks. The emphasis in both was on real time work, as opposed to the batch processing which dominated mainframe usage.

A key architectural difference was the use of a bus. All data moving into and out of a mini travelled along a single path; in contrast, data moved into and out of mainframes along a number of different paths.

Minis were supplied with little in the way of peripherals and software; purchasers were assumed to be competent enough to configure the systems themselves. The emphasis was on bulk sales and on low cost. Minis were truly mini in size, performance and price.

Since that time, minis have taken on mainframe characteristics and vice versa, to the point where the distinction is all but meaningless. Many mainframes today use buses, though often with channels (essentially microprocessors which take some of the I/O processing burden off the central processor) instead of the unintelligent ports found on most minis.

The most powerful mainframes still use channels that are individually connected to the processor, giving a higher I/O rate. One consequence of this architectural difference is that for a given performance, a typical mini will be able to handle a smaller data throughput than a comparable mainframe.

Nonetheless, although today people still regard an IBM 4381 as a mainframe and a DEC VAX as a mini, most users will consider the two as straight competitors.

A quantum leap in the degree of integration of electronic componentry was made in the early seventies with the production of a computer processor on a single chip. This was immediately christened the microprocessor, and computers using them microcomputers.

Microprocessors were initially much less powerful than processors constructed from multiple logic chips, just as minis were originally much less powerful than mainframes. They found two main classes of application: limited complexity process control (as in washing machines) and personal computers. Micros and PCs are often regard as synonymous terms.

Since then micros, too, have evolved and there is no functional distinction between today's 32-bit multi-user micros and a small minicomputer. Furthermore the degree of integration has increased still further, and the day of the single-chip mainframe processor is only two or three years away.

See also: Mainframe generations (page 65).

MAINFRAME GENERATIONS

Processors used in computer systems have gone through four generations of technology.

The first generation, consisting mainly of one-off experimental machines, used thermionic valves for circuitry, many thousands of them in some cases. Main memory was usually constructed using mercury delay lines, though the Manchester University Mark I used a special type of CRT known as a Williams tube. Other first generation systems were Eniac, Edsac, Leo I and Univac I.

The invention of the transistor in 1947 paved the way for the second generation. Use of transistors in place of valves allowed the construction of computers which were more compact, more reliable, dissipated less power and were substantially cheaper.

These advances transformed the computer from a research lab curiosity into a commercial product. IBM entered the computer business in this generation with the 705; so also did Burroughs, General Electric, Honeywell and two precursors of ICL, British Tab and Powers Samas.

The next step was to integrate the components that made up a logic circuit (principally transistors and diodes) into a single circuit. Computers using integrated circuits (ICs) started to appear in the early sixties, and it was during this third generation that computers became commonplace in large organisations.

During the second and third generations, the mercury delay line memories disappeared and ferrite core stores became the standard main memory. This allowed an increase in capacity and thus in the scope of applications that could be handled.

Since then the story has been one of evolution rather than of radical change. The number of integrated circuits that can be mounted on an individual silicon chip (typically of four to six square centimetres) has steadily increased. The term LSI (for large scale integration) was adopted when more than 100 logic circuits could be integrated on a single chip.

As the degree of integration has increased, so the size and price of circuitry has fallen, and computers have become economic for more and more organisations and applications. The term VLSI (for very LSI) was gradually adopted, though there is no general agreement about the dividing line between LSI and VLSI. Today VLSI ICs are found which contain up to a quarter of a million circuits.

Integrated circuitry is also used in main memories, although it was adopted here rather later than in the processor. The pioneer was IBM with the 370 range in 1970, and this is generally taken as the dividing line between the third and fourth generations.

There are two types of silicon transistor used in both logic circuitry and memories – Mos and bipolar. With Mos, the degree of integration is higher, the manufacturing process is simpler. Mos circuits are slower than bipolar circuits, and use less power.

Most circuits are thus used for logic and memory in small computers and PCs. Bipolar circuits are used in large mainframes, many minicomputers and other systems where computational speed is necessary, such as engineering workstations.

Each of these two basic types has several different sub-types. A type of Mos which is becoming increasingly common is Cmos (Complementary Mos). It is characterised by particularly low power consumption.

There are two major types of bipolar circuit, TTL and ECL. TTL (transistor-transistor logic) was for many years the principal logic family used in mainframes, and is still widely used. ECL (emitter-coupled logic) is more powerful, and is thus used in most large mainframes and supercomputers. It requires more power than TTL, and dissipates more heat.

The only alternative to the Mos and bipolar silicon-based technologies is gallium arsenide. Gallium arsenide circuits have not yet been used in any computer system sold in volume, but are considered to have great potential for the future.

See also: Cmos/ECL (page 16), Mainframe, mini, micro (page 62), VLSI (Page 126), and von Neumann architecture (page 128).

MAP/TOP

Open systems interconnection (OSI) is the principle that all systems should be able to communicate and interwork with each other.

This does not imply that there should be only one way of intersystem communication; rather that the various ways in which communication can be established should be internationally standardised.

Two initiatives have been developed to formulate a set of standards (sometimes called a profile) within the overall OSI framework for specific application areas. These are Map (Manufacturing Applications Protocol) and Top (Technical Office Protocol).

An unusual feature is that the driving force in each case has been a user organisation – General Motors for Map, Boeing for Top. Furthermore, they have been strongly supported by other large corporations, and progress in both areas is controlled by user groups.

Map is the earlier of the two: it dates back to 1981, while Top emerged only in 1985. Both have progressed through three versions, with the latest versions appearing in June 1988. The specifications have been frozen for six years, to allow manufacturers and users to invest in products and systems with confidence in their stability.

A lot of commonality exists between the two protocols. They share the same standards for the top five layers of the ISO model, and differ only in the type of local area network used.

Map employs a token ring system using broadband cabling, a choice which reflects the need both for reliability and for high-speed data transfer. Top, in contrast, uses an Ethernet-based baseband configuration.

See also: OSI (page 56).

MERCURY

Mercury Communications is the company licensed by the Government to compete with British Telecom as a provider of telephony and data comms services, both within the UK and internationally.

It owes its existence to the Government's policy of introducing competition in all sectors of the economy. In six years it has built up a turnover of around £100 million and now employs 2,000 people. Mercury moved into profit in 1988.

The company has been gradually building up its range of services. It started with point-to-point leased lines, competing with British Telecom's Datel, Kilostream and Megastream services. Switched services were introduced in 1986.

In the same year Mercury took the first steps towards the introduction of a packet-switched service by purchasing ICL's UK datacomms network. The company entered the public callbox market in 1988.

Mercury was formally launched in June 1981 as a project undertaken by a consortium consisting of Barclays Merchant Bank, BP and Cable & Wireless, in the wake of the Government's deregulation plans for British Telecom.

Its application for a licence was granted in 1982, and subsequently revised to provide more favourable conditions in 1984. In the same year, both Barclays and BP pulled out of the consortium, selling their shares to Cable & Wireless which thus became the sole owner.

Mercury has built a digital trunk network, consisting of 10,000 kilometres of optical fibre linking 30 towns and cities, and supplemented by 3,000 kilometres of microwave links within those towns. This network is now fully interconnected with BT's, so customers need only one telephone to gain access to either or both networks, and are billed only by one company for each call.

Mercury says its network is geared to business users, offering, in comparison with the BT alternative, faster connect time, clearer lines, better security and lower prices.

10000

MIPS

It would be helpful if different computer systems could have their performance rated according to a standard measure. This would enable customers to decide between competing systems on a factual basis, as well as to plan the growth in their configurations against anticipated growth in volume of business.

There have been a number of attempts to develop a uniform measuring rod. But there is a major problem. What the user really needs to know is how quickly a computer will process a given workload.

What a computer actually does is to process instructions, so the problem is to define the given workload in terms of numbers of instructions. This is a non-trivial task. Each job uses a different mix of instructions, and some instructions take more machine cycles to execute than others.

When people first started to measure processor performance in the sixties, they employed statistical techniques to minimise the effect of these variables and produce a performance indicator which showed how fast an "average" workload would be processed.

The best-known of these measures in the UK was the Post Office Work Unit (POWU). ICL described its system performance in POWU measures for a long time, up to and including the introduction of the 2900 series.

Mips (millions of instructions per second) is a generalised form of a POWU which does not relate to a specific benchmark. It theoretically describes how many "average" machine instructions can be executed every second.

Mips came into general use as a measure in the seventies. It is still widely used today, though its limitations have become apparent and the popularity of the measure is now declining.

Two related developments are hastening its decline. They are the growth of multi-tasking – a large mainframe can now process as many as 1,000 different jobs at one time – and the increasing overhead imposed by the operating system. This can be as much as 25% of performance on a multiprocessor system and is around 10% even on a uniprocessor system.

The first factor makes the "average" workload an even more meaningless concept. By tuning of the workload you can significantly improve throughput, even though the performance of the processor is the same.

The second factor increases the amount of non-productive work a processor is doing by a variable amount, which makes quoting a precise mips figures (such as 29.3 mips) worthless. As a result, many commentators are now quoting ranges (eg 27–31 mips).

Although it is reasonably safe to use mips as a measure of comparison of similar systems, such as IBM and IBM-compatible systems, or even mainframes as a whole, it is misleading to compare performance of unlike machines, such as IBM 4381s and DEC VAXes. It is generally reckoned that one VAX mips is worth not much more than half one IBM mips when translated into workload throughput terms.

For the record, sample mips figures for current IBM mainframes are about three for the largest AS/400, about 10 for the largest 4300, about eight for the smallest 3090 and a little over 100 for the six-processor 3090/600S.

Although mips are now gradually falling out of fashion, nearly all manufacturers do quote some measure of performance. DEC and Data General still supply mips figures. Both Unisys-Burroughs and ICL quote relative performance measurements, which are nothing other than mips ratings by another name and using a different scale.

IBM tries to be more exact, using both standardised measures like Linpack (a series of benchmarks designed to measure scientific performance) and proprietary benchmarks like Ramp-C (designed to measure transaction processing performance).

Some suppliers of commercial DP systems, including Honeywell Bull, NCR, Tandem and Unisys-Sperry, are, like IBM with Ramp-C, quoting performance in transactions per second or per hour. Again here you are into problems of defining a "typical" transaction, and they all use different assumptions. In the commercial world, however, transactions per unit of time looks like being the measure that will replace mips as the most popular indicator of performance in the nineties.

NCC

The National Computing Centre (NCC) is a body that fulfills a number of different roles. As the name suggests, one of them is national: it acts as an agent of Government policy in computing. It also functions as a consultancy, a market research organisation, a publisher, a training company and as a vendor of software products.

It is also a membership organisation, with its members – currently around 2,000 – drawn from the ranks of both vendors and users.

The NCC formally came into existence in 1966, though problems in recruiting suitable staff prevented it from starting operations until the following year. It was created as part of the Labour Government's strategy for developing the economy through "the white heat of technology".

From the outset it has played an important part in implementing Government policy. One of its first remits was to tackle the skills shortage, and the major outcome was a course for systems analysts. Graduates received a certificate, and this rapidly became one of the most respected computer qualifications. The course is still run today, and more than 20,000 people now hold the certificate.

The skills shortage is still one of the NCC's priority areas 22 years on. In March 1988 the Centre made its latest contribution to the problem with publication of "The IT Skills Crisis – The Way Ahead".

As a result of its preoccupation with this problem, training has become one of the NCC's most important activities. Among other schemes administered on behalf of the Government, the most notable is probably the Threshold scheme, designed to train school leavers for careers in computing. Starting in 1976, Threshold trained more than 9,000 young people before being superseded by a new scheme in 1987.

The NCC has also been used by the Government to administer

schemes designed to assist the UK computer industry. An example is the Software Products Scheme, launched in 1973 to help the then infant software industry to establish itself in world markets. The Scheme ran for nine years, and was then revived in 1983.

Later in the seventies the NCC was called in to help foster general industry awareness of the micro through the Microprocessor Applications Project (MAP), which provided 25% grants to companies wishing to set up pilot schemes testing the viability of the new microelectronic technology.

At around the same time the NCC established a network of Microsystems Centres, to provide business executives with a place to discuss the usefulness of PCs and their applications.

More recently, Government policy emphasis has been on software engineering. The NCC opened its Software Tools Demonstration Centre in 1986, to promote awareness of the new breed of software development project and to provide a focus for independent assessment.

Alongside this "national" activity, the Centre's commercial operations have steadily grown. A major step was taken in 1968 when it acquired the rights to a software product called Filetab, a file maintenance and report generation product. This proved a gold mine – one of the best-selling products of its type in the UK. In developed, fourth generation form it is still selling well today.

Consultancy, market research and books provide other substantial sources of revenue. More recently, the Centre has built up expertise and a portfolio of software for testing products for conformance to international standards.

As a result, the Centre's revenue mix has changed substantially over its history. In its first year, Government subsidy accounted for 94% of its revenue and commercial activities just 1%. Today commercial activities account for over three-quarters of income, while Government money, now in the form of contracts for services rather than subsidy, has dwindled to 20%.

NON-PROCEDURAL LANGUAGE

Programming languages in common use today – Cobol, Fortran, Basic and the rest – reflect the design principles of the von Neumann type of computer architecture. In essence, they provide programmers with facilities for specifying a sequential series of memory updates.

Each such update destroys the content previously held in that memory location: thus "$x = x+1$" is a statement which destroys the existing value of x, replacing it with a new value. For this reason, programs must be executed sequentially: if you tried to execute separate parts of the program in parallel, you would often be working with incorrect values of variables such as x.

This in turn forces programmers to concentrate on how tasks are to be performed, rather than on what is to be done. This emphasis on the procedures to be followed has led to the generic description "procedural language" for languages such as Cobol and Fortran.

Until quite recently, procedural languages have been virtually the only type of programming language used. Several factors are now forcing a re-think: two are of particular importance.

First, the rising cost of software development relative to hardware costs is becoming a serious limiting factor. It is impractical to sell systems with a hardware cost of hundreds of pounds and a software cost of thousands: some way has to be found of reducing the software cost element. One potential way is to reduce the level of detail that has to be specified.

Second, the need for sequential operation imposes limitations on hardware performance, limitations which are not serious today but are likely to become so during the next decade. In theory, this could be overcome if different processors could operate in parallel on various parts of the task to be performed. Many of the fifth generation research projects around the world are devoted to developing such parallel processing machines.

For these and other reasons, attention is focusing on "non-procedural languages" (also known as "declarative" languages). These languages use some type of logical notation to specify the relationship between the program's starting point and its result, without making any reference to the procedures to be used to move from one to the other.

A key feature (at any rate in theory) is that they are nondestructive. A variable such as x can have only one value throughout a program, and statements such as $x = x+1$ are not permissible.

The two best-known non-procedural languages are Lisp and Prolog. Both are used widely in artificial intelligence work; neither has gained much acceptance in DP circles.

They differ technically in the type of logic used to form equations, and culturally in that Lisp originated in the US, Prolog in France. Thus Lisp tends to predominate in America, Prolog in Europe. MITI (Japan's equivalent of the DTI) has cast its vote in favour of Prolog, making it the prime language for its developing fifth generation computer system.

The arguments in favour of non-procedural languages are attractive enough to have gained a lot of attention. Nonetheless, the potential has yet to be realised in practice, and it remains to be seen whether such a radical departure from traditional computer techniques can produce the hoped-for gains without creating new problems which are at least as great as those besetting traditional programming.

ODA

ODA (Office Document Architecture) is a new communications standard fitting into the top, seventh, layer of the OSI (open systems interconnection) model. It extends the ability to interchange documents between conforming computer systems a significant step further than existing OSI standards such as teletex and X.400.

Teletex is a superior form of telex, with a larger character set and higher transmission speed. X.400 is an electronic mail service. Both are used for the transmission of purely alphanumeric documents or messages that are on receipt displayed or printed out as sent.

In some circumstances, however, additional facilities are required. Many documents contain diagrams or images in addition to text, particularly technical documents. And in many cases, the recipient would like to do further processing before printing.

You might wish to amend a report prepared by a secretary before printing it. Or you might wish to incorporate data sent by a colleague into a letter. Or you might wish to recalculate a spreadsheet according to some different assumptions.

This can be done easily only if the hardware and software of the communicating persons are identical. If you try to amend a document sent to you using a different system from your own, all sorts of problems arise when it comes to reformatting the document for printing.

It is very difficult to ensure that margins and tab positions are set correctly, that diagrams remain embedded in the right part of the text, that footnotes remain on the right page and so on.

The effort involved is in fact so great, and the chance of error so likely, that it is frequently both quicker and easier to type out the revised document from scratch.

The ODA standard has been formulated to overcome these

problems. It standardises the way of transmitting document data – not only text, but diagrams, images and processable data such as spreadsheets.

It also provides for the incorporation of standardised formatting data. Thus in an ODA environment a recipient can edit or amend a document and then print it or retransmit it without having to worry about reformatting.

Before ODA, some mainframe manufacturers had introduced their own proprietary protocols designed to achieve the same objectives. Most notably, IBM introduced DCA (Document Content Architecture).

This led the standards-making bodies to appreciate the need for a vendor-independent standard. After preparatory work by both CCITT (the representative body of the PTTs) and Ecma (European Computer Manufacturers' Association), ISO (the International Standards Organisation) ratified a standard, formally known as "Office Document Architecture and Interchange Format", in 1986.

The ISO standard currently caters only for text documents. Additional sections to cater for graphics, images and data are currently in preparation. This work takes time, and it is unlikely that the full ODA standard will have passed all the ratification stages before 1990.

Nonetheless, systems that conform to those parts of ODA that already exist at various stages of ratification are beginning to appear. At the Hanover Fair in 1988, a group of companies including Bull, ICL, Olivetti and Siemens demonstrated the interchange of ODA documents between their various proprietary systems.

See also: OSI (page 89).

OFFICE AUTOMATION

Office automation developed as a distinct type of computer system in the mid seventies.

Until then, computer applications fell into one of three distinct categories: scientific, process control, and data processing. Data processing – a vague term – was used to mean essentially the automation of the accounts department, and covered applications such as invoicing, payroll and stock control.

The accounts department is itself an office. The first computer specifically designed for data processing, Leo I, was in fact regarded as an office computer – the initial letters stand for Lyons Electronic Office. However, Lyons' terminology didn't catch on, and instead the term "electronic data processing", or EDP, was adopted (this was a variant of "automatic data processing" or ADP, the term used to describe the punched-card-based machines which had been performing the same functions since the turn of the century).

In the seventies, the improvement in cost/performance of basic computer technology had reached the point where practical computers could be placed at the disposal of individuals, rather than being shared by all departments in an organisation. This, in conjunction with the widespread adoption of data communications, made a fundamental change in the pattern of computer usage. The term used to describe this change was "distributed processing".

Distributed processing made possible several other types of computer application: most notably, it made it possible to extend computer power from the accounts department into the other corporate offices. The first realisation of this potential was the specialised word processor, which is simply a personal computer tailored to perform one specific application.

There were very good reasons for applying computer power to office procedures. Clerical costs had been rising as a proportion of overall corporate costs for several decades (and indeed still are). The census returns illustrate the trend: the number of clerical staff rose 50% between 1971 and 1981, during which period the overall working population remained static.

Computers had already been justified for many years in the data processing sector on the basis of staff savings: surely the same gains could be made in other offices? IBM summarised the argument with its sales pitch that for every three numbers processed in the office, there are seven words.

Word processing was an obvious first step: typists form one of the biggest sectors of clerical staff, and almost every office is involved in repetitive typing of one sort or another. But it was not long before the computer industry began to think of the office as a whole.

In the late seventies, therefore, dedicated office automation systems began to appear. They were based on a powerful minis and equipped with a range of generalised software packages. As well as word processing, they included database packages (soon re-named records processing in the office context), diary management, text storage and retrieval, and electronic mail. Spreadsheets followed after they had established themselves in the personal computer market.

The theory looked good, but in practice these large-scale office automation systems were very slow to win market acceptance. In retrospect, the vendors clearly did not appreciate that office automation has distinct differences from data processing.

In the first place, office automation is much more difficult to cost-justify. Some direct cost savings could be made, not only on staff but on paper costs, photocopying bills, courier services and the like. However, these savings usually did not cover the total cost: the difference had to be made up from intangibles such as better selling opportunities, or increased sales from improved customer service – benefits normally summarised under the term competitive advantage.

Second, it became apparent that office automation did not work well unless the system was fully linked with other corporate computer systems – the key word is integration. Records processing is not much use unless you can access the corporate database.

Third, office automation is a set of tools rather than a "load-and-go" packaged solution. Users need to do a lot of careful planning to make sure they gain the benefit from their investment, and this invariably involves a substantial training programme.

Over the past few years, these problems have become more clearly recognised. In addition, the mainframe manufacturers have now joined the market, which has had a stimulating effect, and the open systems interconnection (OSI) standards have begun to appear, making integration easier. As a result, office automation is now a practical reality.

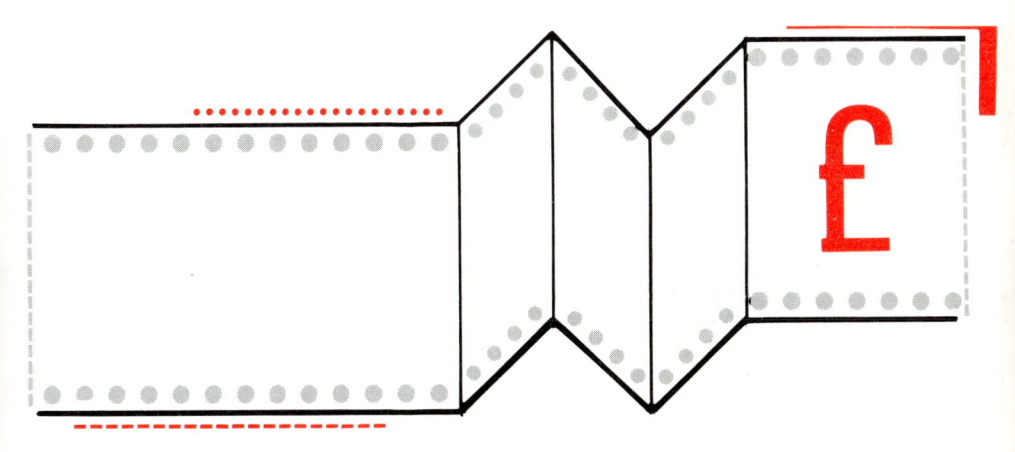

OPTICAL COMPUTING

Apart from the 19th Century attempts by Babbage to build computers from purely mechanical components, and the electromechanical differential analysers of the early 20th Century, all computers have relied on electronics for their implementation. Over the past decade, however, interest has been developing in the possibilities of building optical computers.

The principle is that you use laser beams instead of electricity to switch data bits on and off. This offers the potential of a quantum leap in switching speed.

The breakthrough which sparked off the present research into optical computing came in 1974 with the discovery by Bell Labs that crystals can exist in two states, one of which lets in much more light than the other. These two states can be made to represent the zeroes and ones of binary arithmetic, so the crystals can be used as switches. The phenomenon is known as crystal bistability. (Since then it has been discovered that some crystals can have more than two states. This opens up the intriguing possibility of constructing a computer which uses a base numbering system other than binary.)

The Bell Labs discovery triggered off research efforts in many other organisations, both commercial and academic. They include Heriot-Watt University, which has established a reputation in the forefront of the field.

In 1984 the EEC Commission was sufficiently impressed by the potential of optical computing to allocate £1.2 million funding to a research project known as the European Optical Bistability Project, coordinated by Heriot-Watt University and involving eight research teams in six European countries.

This project produced the world's first optical circuits capable of demonstration, an event that happened at the 1986 Hanover Fair.

From circuits to fully fledged computers could take a comparatively short time. Heriot-Watt has predicted that specialised computational systems might be available as early as 1991, with full general-purpose systems coming after another five years.

As well as providing a new technology for computer processors, optical switches could also revolutionise display terminals. The EEC Commission has again been active, funding a £500,000 project.

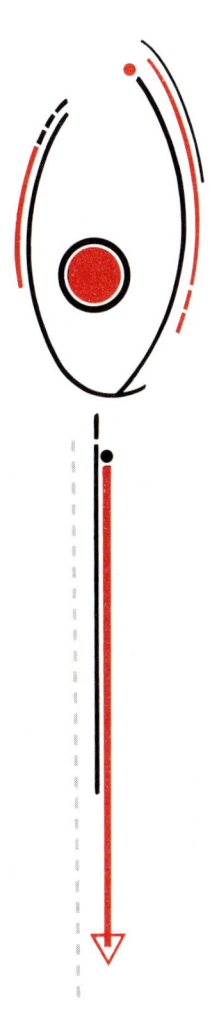

OPTICAL DISC

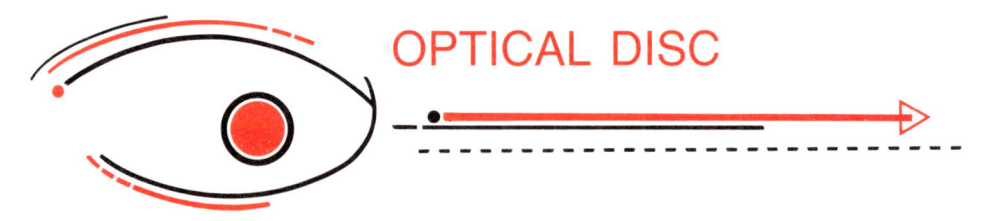

Since the early days of computer history, computer subsidiary storage devices have employed magnetic recording techniques. Magnetic tapes, discs, drums and cards have between them had far superior price/performance characteristics than the alternatives.

As computers have become a more integral part of corporate planning and decision-making, so the volume of data stored both on- and off-line has increased. At the same time, the packing density of magnetic recording technology has also been increasing, but at a significantly slower rate.

We can put numbers to this. It has been estimated that the areal packing density of magnetic discs has been increasing at a rate of 6% per annum throughout the eighties. Data storage requirements in large installations are currently increasing at an average of 10 times this amount.

The disparity looks set to grow for at least the next decade. Natural language fifth generation computers will impose storage requirements one or two orders of magnitude greater than today.

The result, from the user's point of view, is a growing floor-space problem. As computing usage grows, so you need more and more square metres to house your disc and tape equipment.

The problem has focused attention on alternative ways of storing data, and of these, optical disc technology is currently the most promising.

The principle is that instead of using a magnet to effect a change in polarity in a magnetically sensitive recording surface, you use a laser beam to effect an optically detectable change in a light-sensitive surface.

Laser beams are used because, unlike ordinary light beams (as from a torch or a car headlamp) they are parallel-sided. As a result, they can be focused with quite extraordinary accuracy – it's no problem at all to project one on to a small mirror sitting on a oscillating object a quarter of a million miles away.

This quality of the laser beam allows us to measure exactly how far away the moon is. Applied to the more immediately relevant problem of storage media, it permits a very high packing density, up to 10 times that of the most advanced magnetic disc available today.

The same quality means that the distance between the light source and the recording surface is comparatively irrelevant.

With magnetic read/write heads, there is a direct relationship between the "flying height" and the packing density – the further the distance from the surface, the lower the density. Thus read/write heads on disc drives have to be as close as possible to the disc – a few millionths of an inch away.

This creates great engineering complexity as well as the possibility of a head crash. Optical disc systems are inherently easier to engineer as well as more reliable.

These qualities have been recognised for a long time. They have not led to optical storage systems for computers before now because of the difficulty of developing a practicable read/write technology. This difficulty has not yet been overcome.

The optical disc systems available today are write-once – they are sometimes referred to as Worm devices (write once, read many). The act of writing makes a permanent, irreversible change in the recording surface. The laser beam literally burns a hole in the medium.

These write-once systems are used for archival purposes, especially where security is paramount. They compete more with paper and microfilm storage systems than with computer-based systems, though they are coming to be seen as an alternative to magnetic tape.

Products of this type have been available since the mid-eighties. IBM gave the concept its approval by announcing a Worm product for use with the PS/2 in April 1987.

Capacities of such products are much larger than on magnetic discs. The current maximum is 2Gb, recorded on both sides of a single 12" platter. Discs with a diameter of 5.25" are also offered, typically with capacities of 200Mb (as in the IBM product) to 800Mb. These yield prices of less than 50p per megabyte stored, compared with prices of around £15 per megabyte on Winchester discs. Access time is much slower, however, at 100 to 150 milliseconds or more.

A special type of write-once optical disc is the CD-Rom. CD-Roms are written to once only, but this happens before they reach the user (like Mos Roms in personal computers). They are sold with pre-recorded information, just as music compact discs are sold with pre-recorded sound.

Write-once systems clearly cannot substitute for magnetic discs. Read/write systems may be just around the corner, however. Philips, in conjunction with Du Pont Optical, announced a 5.25" product in October 1988 in the US, and will be bringing it to Europe in 1989. Several other companies are also said to be on the verge of making product launches.

The real question mark hanging over these products concerns the access time. If the manufacturers can get anywhere close to 30 milliseconds, the magnetic disc would be under real threat.

OPTICAL FIBRE

Optical fibre is a new technology used for the transmission of electrical signals. It permits the transmission of information by making a beam of light travel within a glass filament of microscopic dimensions, about the size of a human hair. The light source is either a light-emitting diode or a laser.

Optical fibre is superior in a number of important respects to conventional copper-based transmission cabling, and promises to be one of the principal driving forces behind IT development over the next decade.

The principle of using light as a means of transmitting signals down a communications line was recognised in the last century, and was demonstrated using a jet of water at a meeting of the Royal Society in the 1870s. The enabling technology did not exist then, and the idea of using glass fibres is naturally more recent: it dates to 1966, when two researchers at STC published a paper on the subject.

British Telecom became interested in the seventies, conducting experiments which led to widescale implementation of the technology during the eighties. The Government recognised the potential of fibre optics in 1982, when it published a report under the auspices of the Information Technology Advisory Panel. This stimulated industry interest which has continued ever since.

At the time the STC paper was published, the major problem was signal attenuation (the rate at which the signal being transmitted fades, which in turn determines the distance at which it is necessary to refresh the signal).

In those days, when attenuation was over 500 decibels per kilometre, STC estimated that optical fibre would not be of any practical use unless the rate of signal loss could be reduced to 20 dB/km. That seemed a very remote goal at the time, but developments in the construction of fibre optic cables enabled the target to be reached within a few years, and the current threshold is well under 1 dB/km.

That has allowed the length of cable between repeater stations to be extended to the point where, in April 1988, British Telecom set a new record for the world's longest cable, a 126 km stretch between Britain and Ireland.

The major advantages of optical fibre over conventional copper cabling are, first, a substantial increase in maximum transmission speed (it is nearly twice as fast); second, environmental characteristics (it is easy to install, is much lighter, and occupies less space); and third, the absence of electromagnetic interference.

The major disadvantages are first, cost (currently between two and three times as much) and second, the need for specialist skills to maintain the cabling.

These characteristics influence the applications where optical fibre is used. A well-known example is the British Telecom trunk network: the corporation has been converting the trunk cabling to optical fibre since 1980, and has now installed over 200,000 kilometres. Optical fibre currently handles about 55% of all trunk routings. The transmission speed is 565 Mbits per second.

Optical fibre is likely to take over as the usual medium for connecting mainframes to high-speed peripherals, such as disc drives, in the near future. ICL showed the way in 1985, when it announced Macrolan disc drive connections for its Series 39 mainframes, with a transmission speed of 50 Mbits per second over distances of up to 1.5 kms. IBM is developing optical fibre cabling for its next generation of mainframes.

OSI

OSI stands for Open Systems Interconnection, the buzz-phrase which describes the utopia whereby computer systems of all kinds can interwork with each other using communications lines.

At present this is far from being the case. Not only do different suppliers use different data communications protocols, but quite often two systems of different generations from the same supplier are not compatible with each other.

Interworking between incompatible devices involves use of intermediary translation devices such as protocol converters. These add to the cost for the user, as well as making communication more inefficient.

The initiative to overcome this problem has come from the International Standards Organisation (ISO). Its first act was to split up the various individual components of a communication into a hierarchy of layers – the well-known seven-layer model.

This is not a standard in itself, but a framework within which future standards work could proceed.

Much of the preliminary work in OSI standards-making has been done by bodies that are junior in status – CCITT, Ecma, and IEEE. Their efforts have made a substantial contribution to the shape of the ISO standards that are in existence today.

Standards from either the ISO or the other bodies exist now for all seven layers. However, there is still some way to go before open systems interconnection can be truly said to be a reality.

Partly this is because it is not possible to specify an optimum way of performing the functions specified in each layer. To cater for all types of communication and application, there will need to be several different standards per layer.

See also: Map/Top (page 67), ODA (page 77), X.25 (page 135), and X.400 (page 137).

PARALLEL PROCESSING

Nearly all computers today operate serially: they perform one operation on one item of data at a time, completing that operation before starting the next. Multitasking systems do not infringe this principle: here individual operations making up one task are interleaved with those of another so as to give the impression that two jobs are executed at the same time.

The time gap between the completion of one operation and the next is so small – a tiny fraction of a second – that serial operation has not seriously inhibited the use of computers up to now. The most powerful mainframes today are capable of processing 1,000-plus interactive terminal conversations simultaneously and providing an acceptable response time for each.

However, the increase in user demand for computer power has for some time now been outstripping the rate of technical progress. Processor performance is improving at a rate of 15%-20% a year. User demand is growing at two to three times this rate.

This has created a problem for the designers of large mainframes, which has been temporarily overcome by developing multiprocessor systems. Many large mainframes today have two processors, while the very largest have four or six.

There is a limit to how long this can continue. Every time you add another processor, you increase the amount of communication necessary between them to ensure that the system operates effectively, and thus decrease the amount of power available for processing. The law of diminishing returns operates: eventually, you gain no increase in power at all.

So there is pressure to find another way of increasing system performance. Parallel processing gives, in theory at least, an unlimited performance gain, so the concept is currently attracting great attention.

Parallel processing of a limited kind has been performed for many years by array processors. These do perform operations on more than one item of data at a time, but can execute only one instruction at a time.

For some applications, principally scientific ones, array processors provide substantial increases in performance when compared to conventional fourth generation computers. For data processing applications, true parallel processing is necessary, and this is one of the objectives of the various fifth generation development programmes.

True parallel processing involves linking processors together in such a way that each processor can perform different operations on different data at the same time. This allows individual jobs to be run faster, assuming they have some intrinsic degree of parallelism.

A payroll application does, for example. For any one individual, you naturally cannot compute net pay until you have worked out the gross pay, the tax and the other deductions. But there is no reason, in principle, why you should not calculate the gross pay for every individual on the payroll in parallel, and then perform each of the subsequent calculations in parallel as well.

There are obvious problems to be overcome before this can be done, such as making all the data available to the system simultaneously, and reorganising the software to perform the calculations in parallel. But the theoretical gains in performance, particularly in applications with a large computational content, are such that much work is being carried out to resolve the difficulties.

Parallel processing computers have in the last few years begun to form a recognisable market sector of their own, though there are still as yet comparatively few in operation. They are sold mainly to customers with highly compute-intensive applications, and fall into two classes.

In the first kind, there is a relatively small number of processors – typically up to eight – communicating with each other via an interprocessor bus. Main memory is also linked to the bus, and is thus shared by the processors. Companies marketing systems of this kind include Alliant, Convex, ETA Systems and Sequent.

In the second kind, a very large number of small processors – up to tens of thousands – each with its own memory is linked to each adjacent processor in a configuration known as a hypercube. A hypercube has n dimensions. If n is equal to six, then each processor is linked to the adjacent six processors.

Companies marketing this type of system include NCube, Floating Point Systems and Meiko. The last two companies use the Inmos Transputer as the individual processor.

There is considerable argument about which arrangement is best. The general consensus seems to be that hypercube systems have the biggest growth potential, while bus systems are simpler and cheaper to design.

See also: Vector processing (page 120).

PICK

Pick is a multi-user operating system which, like Unix, is available on a wide variety of systems ranging from personal computers to mainframes. Unlike Unix, however, Pick has its own integral database management system, and is designed for use by people with no programming experience.

Pick is named after its developer, Dick Pick, whose company Pick Systems has licensed its use to about 30 different vendors. Pick first appeared in the early seventies, and was introduced to the UK in 1975 by CMC, acting as distributor for Microdata.

The UK is now the biggest market for the system outside the US, with some 3,000 installations. Microdata's successor, McDonnell Douglas, is still the market leader here today. Its operating system, called Reality, is a superset of Pick.

Other Pick licensees have also developed their own version, with added functionality, and this has caused compatibility concerns. There are about 3,000 packages available worldwide for use with Pick systems, and it is clearly an advantage both to end-users and software developers if they can be run on all Pick systems.

This led a group of Pick licensees to band together and form a body known as the Spectrum Manufacturers' Association. A major objective of the Association is to develop an agreed standard version of Pick, though this has yet to appear.

The Association is a US-based organisation. British Pick vendors have their own body, the Pick Forum, formed in 1986.

Pick has been constantly updated since it was first released. Originally, the different versions were known by their year of introduction; thus the 1980 version was known as Release 80.

In 1984 however, R84 was rechristened Open Architecture Version 1.0. This was superseded in 1987 by Version 2.0, usually abbreviated to OA2.

Pick is often contrasted with Unix, as both are aiming at the same market. There are two major differences between them.

Unix is backed by the financial might of AT&T, while Pick is essentially the work of one man. Unix has thus gained much greater publicity, and is installed on many more sites.

The second difference is in appeal: Unix is popular with academics and with committed computer professionals such as systems programmers, while Pick appeals more to applications programmers and even end-users.

This is because Pick is, by general consent, much the easier of the two to use. This characteristic has become more important with the advent of personal computing, which has taught users the value of having control over their own computing activities without needing to refer to a central IT department.

For this reason Pick, though always likely to have less market penetration than Unix, looks assured of maintaining its own niche in the market.

PROTOCOL

A protocol is a set of rules governing the formatting of data transmitted between computers, and/or terminals. A protocol may be proprietary (such as IBM 3270, DEC VT100, British Telecom Prestel), or the result of a formalised standards-making procedure (like IEEE 488, X.25).

Protocols are needed because a string of zeroes and ones emerging from a data communications line is not very meaningful in itself. You need to know the coding system employed by the sending device before you can understand it.

It is not just a question of coding. Every transmission contains some information which is not part of the message.

Part of this additional information will be routing instructions, another part security codes inserted to ensure that the message which reaches your end is the same as the message which left the sender.

None of these procedures is the subject of a universal standard. Different conventions are adopted depending on the nature of the application and the type of transmission.

In addition, vendors have a vested interest in non-standardisation: it locks in their users and so ensures additional revenues.

RELATIONAL DATABASE

A relational database management system (RDBMS) is a type of DBMS that emerged in the seventies, and is now superseding the predecessor DBMS systems. Relational systems have been launched by nearly all the major computer manufacturers during the past five years.

The RDBMS was designed to overcome the limitations of conventional DBMS in handling the very large transaction processing databases that were being developed.

In earlier hierarchical and networked database systems, the relationship between data items is defined by pointers. There are two consequences of this type of organisation: first, each database needs to be reorganised quite frequently as new types of data are added; and second, there is a natural limit to the size of the database.

In addition, access to the data is typically by means of relatively low-level commands. These factors inhibit the degree to which the database can be understood and used by non-technical users, which has proved a grave disadvantage as applications involving user interrogation of databases have grown.

The RDBMS overcomes these drawbacks by using a different method to set up the database. It makes use of the relational model, a mathematical concept first described by Edgar Codd of IBM in 1970. Codd has summarised the characteristics of an RDBMS in a set of 12 rules, first published in October 1985. He expanded these rules into a more comprehensive set of 166, grouped in 13 classes, in 1987.

A major feature of the relational model is that data is organised in the form of tables, consisting of rows and columns.

While the RDBMS overcomes the major problems inherent in the earlier database systems, it brings some new ones of its own. Performance still, in the view of many specialists, compares unfavourably.

To improve performance, most developers have adopted a modified version of Codd's model, which has led to arguments about the "purity" of the various systems available. No system yet sold, in fact, fulfills all the requirements of the 12 original rules.

This is partly a consequence of novelty; the investment in development in RDBMS is as yet considerably less than that in the earlier systems.

IBM has itself built on Codd's work and introduced a number of different RDBMS. The first system was SQL/DS, for mainframes running under VM, while a second system called DB/2, for MVS mainframes, was introduced in 1983 and is now promoted as a major strategic product by the company.

Relational DBMS from independent software developers that have sold well include Ingres, Oracle and Rapport for mainframes, and dBase-II and III for personal computers.

See also: Database (page 21), SQL (page 105).

rdbms

RISC

It is the goal of all computer system designers to increase system performance. This stimulates the market by allowing existing users to increase the work done for the same cost, by bringing in new users who could not previously afford computing, and by opening up new applications which were not previously economic.

Increases in system performance are usually fuelled by developments in the underlying technologies. If the switching speed of the basic logic circuits is quicker, overall performance is naturally improved.

There is another way, however, and that is to devise a better way of making the system operate. If less switching needs to be done to achieve a given result, overall performance will again improve. Riscs (reduced instruction set computers) are a case in point.

The essence of the problem addressed by Riscs is that programs are written in high-level languages, and the high-level language source code statements have to be translated into machine code before work can take place.

Conventional computers achieve this by having large instruction sets to match the complexity of high-level languages: thus every source code statement is translated directly by the compiler into one instruction in the set.

These instructions are then broken down into several smaller steps – or microinstructions – before execution. Thus a number of machine cycles is required to execute each instruction.

Riscs start from the assumption that most of the instructions in these large instruction sets are very rarely used. Accordingly, they employ a much smaller set of only the most commonly used instructions, typically a half to a fifth in size.

As a result, they do away with the need for microcoded logic and allow each instruction to be executed in a single cycle.

There is a trade-off between these two alternatives. Conventional systems incur a performance overhead in the need for translation of architectural instructions into microinstructions. Riscs avoid this overhead, but incur another one whenever an instruction outside the machine instruction set is encountered, as this then has to be translated into several instructions within it.

The determining factor therefore is how many complex instructions are encountered in executing a workload. The greater the number, the more efficient conventional architecture will be; the lesser the number, the more efficient Riscs will be. This in turn is determined by the workload.

Many Riscs are aimed at specific scientific and technical applications, where the number of different instructions encountered is minimised by the nature of the application, and in particular the I/O handling requirement is small.

Riscs began to appear in the early eighties. At first they were sold by new companies, of which the most successful has been Pyramid Technology.

IBM legitimised the Risc concept with the introduction of the 6150 scientific workstation early in 1986. Hewlett-Packard announced its Risc-based Precision Architecture to the world a month later, saying that all its future systems will conform to this design.

The commitment of these two companies opened the floodgates, and over the past two years many other companies have launched products or at least announced Risc developments.

One of the most influential has been Sun Microsystems, which is attempting to make its proprietary Sparc (Scalable Processor ARChitecture) design an industry standard. It has issued licences to a number of companies including AT&T and ICL.

SAA

Systems Application Architecture (SAA), announced by IBM in March 1987, is widely held to be the most important strategic initiative from the company since the launch of Systems Network Architecture (SNA) in 1974.

SAA is essentially a set of procedures designed to standardise the interface between programs (both utilities and applications) and the outside world (including users, other programs and operating systems).

This will provide, in IBM's own words, "a framework for productively designing and developing applications with cross-systems consistency".

In other words, an SAA product designed to run on one of IBM's three major architectures (PS/2, AS/400 and 370) will be able to be ported, with only minor modification, to both the other two.

This has benefits for users running networks incorporating systems of different IBM architectures; for third-party software developers; and for IBM itself.

Standardising on the user interface (including menus, error messages, the meaning of function keys) will bring other benefits. Users who have mastered any application will quickly be able to come to terms with any other.

By no means all current IBM products will be brought within the SAA framework. IBM has announced no plans to cater for products outside its three major architectures, such as the 6150 Risc computer, the Series 1 mini and the System 88 fault-tolerant system.

Major software products excluded include IMS, TSO and Basic. RPG and PL/I were also excluded from the original announcement, but IBM has since indicated it might change its mind.

The SAA framework is split by IBM into three elements: Common User Access; Common Programming Interface; and Common Communications Support.

Common User Access defines the basic elements of the user interface – screen layouts, menus, keyboard layouts – and how to achieve them.

Common Communications Support specifies the rules covering communications between SAA programs and networks. It is based on extensions to existing data communications architectures including SNA.

Common Programming Interface consists of the languages and services needed to develop applications. The languages are C, Cobol and Fortran; an application generator based on Cross System Product (CSP): and a command language based on Rexx (the JCL used with VM). The services are the Database Interface (based on SQL), the Screen Interface (based on ez-vu) and the Query Interface (based on QMF).

SNA

Systems Network Architecture is IBM's blueprint for constructing information processing networks from IBM products. It consists of three elements.

First, SNA describes the logical structure used in configuring IBM networks. Second, it specifies the formats, protocols and operational sequences used for transmitting data through a network. Third, it consists of a set of products which conform to the structure and implement the rules.

The need for a network architecture arose out of the distributed data processing trend of the mid-seventies. By putting intelligence in terminals and workstations, computing networks became much more complex and difficult to work with.

A network architecture simplifies the job of building such networks. Its housekeeping routines minimise the problems of installation, enhancement, management and maintenance, and it obviates the need for programmers to consider the network configuration when developing applications programs.

IBM was the first of the major computer manufacturers to introduce a network architecture, launching SNA in 1974, and billing it then as its most important single announcement since the launch of the 360 mainframe series a decade earlier.

This claim recognised the growing importance of the distributed data processing market. It also revealed SNA as a defensive strategic counter to the threat posed by the minicomputer manufacturers to IBM's market position.

SNA offered IBM users some of the advantages provided by the low-cost mini, while allowing them to maintain their existing commitment to mainframe computing – the major source of IBM's revenues.

SNA is often spoken of as a *"de facto* standard". In fact it is not internationally standardised: it is controlled wholly by IBM which reserves the right to change any part of it at any time.

Here it contrasts with the open systems interconnection (OSI) standards currently being formulated by the standards-making bodies, particularly CCITT, Ecma, IEEE and ISO.

Since these standards are arrived at by a process of gradually working towards a consensus, they take much longer to establish than decisions made by a single company. Once completed, however, they are more stable: changing them takes just as much work as creating them in the first place.

See also: LU 6.2 (page 60).

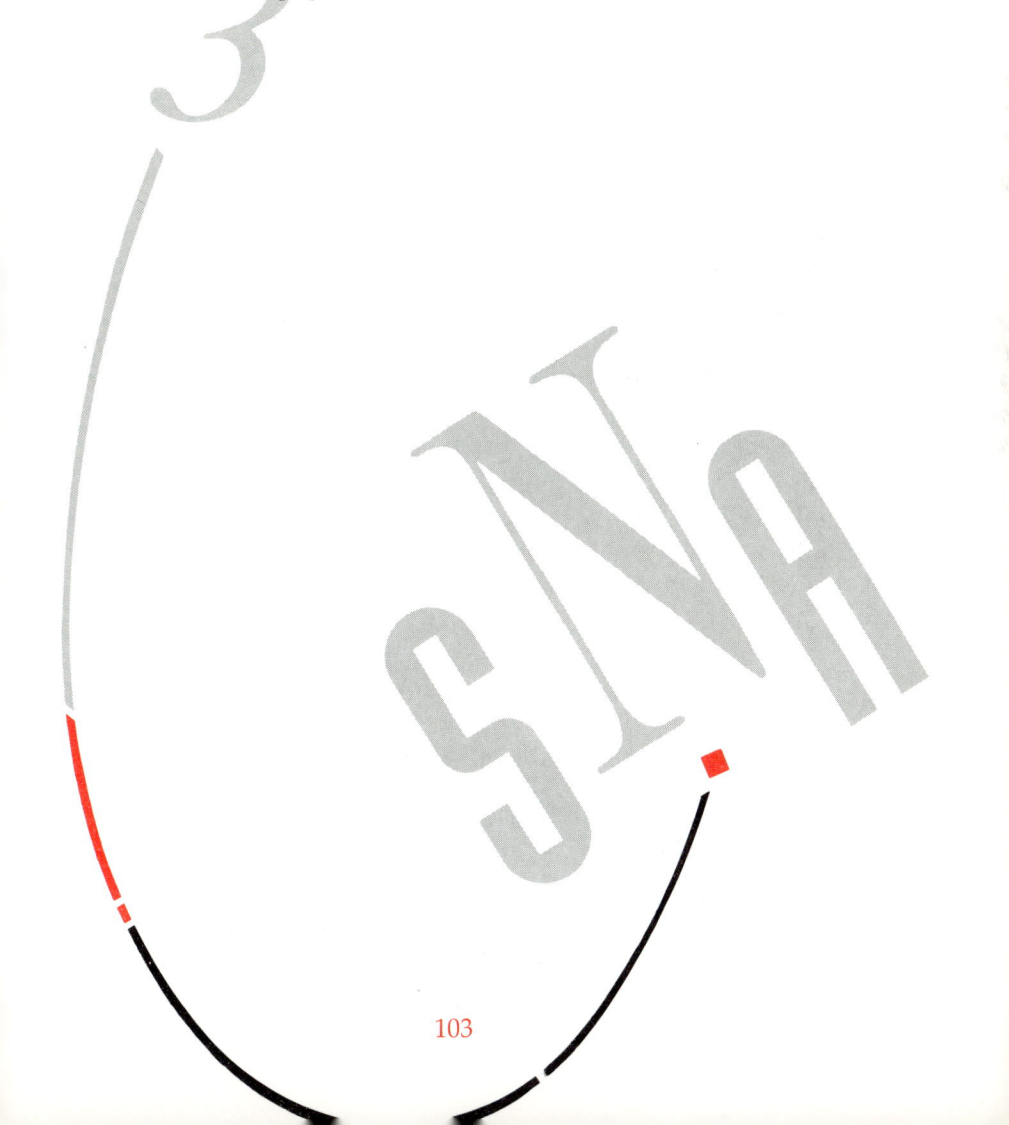

SPREADSHEET

A spreadsheet is a type of packaged program which facilitates the manipulation of interdependent rows and columns of data.

This simple concept has proved a remarkably useful tool for budgetary control and financial modelling.

A spreadsheet allows you to construct a budget in such a way that the relationship between one item of data and another can be specified.

For example, if you change the figure for wages per hour, the system will immediately calculate the resulting figures for the cost of production, the relative percentage cost of labour and the profit margin.

This facility is useful in two ways. Operationally, it allows you to see immediately the effect of a change such as a union-negotiated increase in wage rates, and to take appropriate action such as deciding on the level of product price increase.

Strategically, you can test the impact of a number of different assumptions, and then select the most favourable option.

Historically, the spreadsheet dates to the late seventies, It was one of the two applications that fuelled the personal computer boom (the other was word processing).

At a stroke it took financial modelling away from the timesharing companies, with the accompanying costly line and connect charges, and put it on users' desks.

Spreadsheet systems were originally standalone packages – the most successful of the early ones was Visicalc.

In the early eighties, they began to be integrated with other applications, most notably word processing and graphics, so that the output from a spreadsheet could be incorporated in a letter or turned into a graph. The most successful of the integrated packages has been Lotus Development's 1-2-3.

SQL

SQL is a standardised high-level access language used by programmers to write routines for querying relational databases.

Originally developed by IBM in 1973 under the name Structured English Query Language (Sequel), it was developed over the next couple of years in conjunction with IBM's prototype relational database system, System R. The result was a revised version, Sequel 2, which was subsequently christened SQL (for Structured Query Language).

Curiously, the first product to become available for use with SQL came not from IBM, but from Oracle. IBM has since introduced two relational database systems that use SQL: the confusingly named SQL/DS for systems running VM and DOS/VSE, and DB2 for MVS systems.

IBM has emphasised its commitment to SQL by naming it as the standard query language in its Systems Application Architecture (SAA). Other vendors have also released SQL products, to the point where it has now become a *de facto* standard.

This has led the standards-making bodies to consider formulation of a *de jure* standard. ANSI was first in the field, and its SQL standard was ratified in 1986. ISO followed, and its SQL standard (reference IS 9075) completed the ratification stages in 1987. (It has since been published by the BSI, reference BS 6964.) These standards do not cover all facilities needed in an access language. Notably, they do not cater for referential integrity: that is, they do not specify the facilities necessary to ensure internal consistency of the database.

These omissions were not accidental; it was considered important to get a standard out as soon as possible, and so influence systems designers and vendors at the earliest possible stage, rather than take longer and produce a full facilities standard at the outset.

Draft versions of updates to both the ANSI and ISO standards, referred to as SQL 2, have now been published.

See also: Relational database (page 96).

SUPERCONDUCTIVITY

Conductivity – the ability to conduct electricity – is a quality possessed by a large number of substances. The extent to which a material conducts electricity is determined by the power of resistance of its component atoms to the current flow. If resistance is low, conductivity is high, and vice versa.

In some materials, the component atoms offer no resistance to the current flow at all. Once the current is switched on, it flows through the material freely and without hindrance. This phenomenon is called superconductivity.

Such materials are potentially extremely useful. Overcoming electrical resistance requires power, which costs money. Great savings could be made in the operation of electrical devices if they could be built from superconducting materials.

Resistance generates heat. That heat needs to be dissipated, which is why powerful computers need expensive cooling systems, and require an air-conditioned environment. In addition, the heat generation imposes a limit on the number of devices which can be integrated on the same chip, and accounts for a power loss of up to 15%.

In theory, therefore, superconducting materials are ideal for computer systems – they'd be cheaper to run, and could be made much more powerful. But there is a snag.

The ability to superconduct comes only into operation when the materials used are cooled to very low temperatures. Until recently, the highest temperature at which any material could be made to superconduct was 23° Kelvin (degrees above absolute zero), which equals −250° Centigrade. Typical superconducting temperatures were in the range 10 to 15° K.

That is far colder than anywhere on earth – to find such temperatures in nature you have to venture out into space. And to achieve these temperatures at all on earth you have to use liquid helium. Helium is one of the scarcest elements on earth, and is very expensive (liquid helium costs around £300 a kilogram).

None the less, the potential offered by superconductors is such that many companies have spent time and money trying to develop practical superconducting devices. The most famous such research effort came from IBM, which spent $100 million trying to develop a superconducting logic circuit with a switching speed of under 10 picoseconds before abandoning the attempt in 1983.

This circuit is known as a Josephson junction (named after Brian Josephson, the British scientist who invented it). Josephson junctions switch quickly between a superconducting state and a state of low conductivity (high resistance), and these states can be taken to represent the zeroes and ones of binary arithmetic.

Paradoxically, it was IBM which made the discovery that has aroused the present fever-pitch excitement. In 1986, two scientists at the company's Zurich research lab, Georg Bednorz and Alex Mueller, discovered a new class of superconductors formed from ceramic compounds.

These compounds differ from the previously known superconductors (made from niobium and tin) in operating at significantly higher temperatures. The first one discovered operated at 35° K. Since then, research labs all over the world have been experimenting with different materials to try to raise the "transition threshold" still further.

The threshold quickly jumped from 35° K to 90° K. Going above 77° K was an important breakthrough, as it allowed the use of liquid nitrogen as the cooling agent.

Since then the threshold has risen further still. A major landmark was reached in March 1988, when Cambridge University announced it had developed a material that would superconduct at less than minus 100° C (173 degrees K).

The research centre at Cambridge had been established only two months earlier, as a result of a British Government decision to put more money into superconductivity research.

Translating these laboratory discoveries into working commercial products will take some time. IBM, mindful of the failure of its Josephson junction programme, has said it is not trying to develop superconducting logic products; it is concentrating instead on developing connecting links to be used within a computer.

Cambridge University disagrees, announcing in 1987 that it had built a simple Josephson junction logic switch from one of the new ceramic compounds. Stanford University in California made a similar announcement at around the same time.

It is unlikely that these and other research programmes will produce saleable products within 10 years. Superconducting computers are therefore unlikely to appear before the end of the century.

TELETEX

Teletex is an internationally standardised method of sending text messages and documents between computer systems. The teletex standards were ratified by CCITT (the representative body for the world's Post, Telegraph & Telephone Administrations) in 1980. A UK service was introduced by British Telecom in 1985.

Teletex was formulated as a replacement for the antiquated telex network, and allows word processors and terminals conforming to the standard to exchange messages with any other conforming system anywhere in the world.

Teletex is superior to telex in a number of respects. First, it has a much more extensive character set. Telex is limited to upper-case characters, numbers and punctuation marks, while the teletex set has 366 characters, including not only lower case but accents, other character-related symbols and a limited number of graphics symbols.

Second, teletex is not restricted to a single special-purpose network, but can be used on any public data communications network.

Third, it is very much quicker: speeds vary depending on the network used, but start at 2.4Kbits per second, compared with the standard 50 bits per second for telex (roughly, 3,500 wpm against 80 wpm).

Fourth, it makes provision for some elements of presentation, including indentation, centred headings, tabs and underlining.

Because of these advantages it was expected that teletex would replace telex sometime in the 1990s. This now seems unlikely to happen.

Growth in teletex usage has been slow. The reason is that teletex has been superseded by progress in other communications services, notably fax (which allows transmission of images as well as text) and X.400 electronic mail.

The choice of the word "teletex" for this new service was a bad one, as it is easily confused with the quite different concept "teletext". Teletext is the term used to describe broadcast videotex services such as Ceefax and Oracle.

See also: X.400 (page 137)

THIN-FILM HEAD

The last major development in magnetic disc drive technology was the thin-film head, introduced by IBM and used in its current 3380 range disc drives.

Thin-film heads differ from their predecessors in that the magnets in the read/write head are manufactured out of sputtered films of copper, rather than being made from a coil of copper wire. The reduction in magnet size allows the magnetic domains created by the heads to be substantially smaller and thus the packing density of the media to be greater.

This greater density is necessary to improve cost/performance and thus to meet user demand for increasingly more powerful systems at an economic cost. This demand has been satisfied over the 30 years of disc drive history by a series of radical innovations at roughly five-year intervals, followed by a period of development and exploitation of each one.

The last four of these innovations have been the ferrite core head of the 2314 in the mid-sixties (drive capacity 29 Mbytes); the voice coil motor of the 3330 in 1970 (capacity 100 Mbytes): the adoption of fixed discs in sealed units as in the 3350 of 1975 (capacity 317 Mbytes); and the thin-film head as used in the 3380 of 1980 (capacity 1,260 Mbytes).

These four innovations have thus been responsible for maintaining the annual average increase in packing density of the 15-year period at about 30%. The progression suggests we are due for another quantum leap any time now, and most commentators are predicting that this will be the adoption of vertical recording techniques.

Ever since the introduction of the disc drive, IBM has enjoyed technical leadership in disc technology. A consequence has been that disc drives have accounted for an increasingly larger share of both sales and profits.

TOKEN RING

Token ring is a term defining a type of network architecture which uses a token passing transmission protocol. It describes a data communications network configured in the form of a ring (as opposed to a star or tree), wherein transmissions between network nodes are controlled by the circulation of a token – a specified unique pattern of bits – around the ring.

Whenever the token passes a node, that node is authorised to make any transmissions that it wishes. The node also checks any messages circulating round the ring to see if its address is on any of them, and if so reads those messages. Once that node has completed sending and receiving, the token passes around the ring to the next node.

The token passing protocol is one of two commonly used in local area networks (Lans); the other is carrier sense multiple access/collision detection (CSMA/CD). Under CSMA/CD a node on a network wishing to transmit a message first checks to ensure that no other node is doing so before starting transmission.

In this situation it is possible for two nodes to start transmitting simultaneously, and if that happens the two messages could find themselves competing for the same transmission path at the same time (an impossible situation in a token-passing system).

To avert the chaotic results which could follow, a special monitoring procedure is incorporated to detect such collisions and to cause the nodes involved to stop transmissions until the line becomes free.

Both types of protocol have been standardised by the Institute of Electrical and Electronic Engineers (IEEE). CSMA/CD is used in Ethernet systems, which are currently the most widely used type of Lan. Token passing was introduced by Datapoint in its Arcnet system, one of the most popular of the pioneer Lan systems which was used to link Datapoint minis.

It has since been adopted by IBM in its own proprietary PC network system, called Token Ring and announced in October 1985. IBM Token Ring uses specially developed IBM cabling of the copper twisted pair type, and can support both voice and data simultaneously. It currently has a maximum transmission speed of 4 Mbits per second.

Since the launch, IBM has elevated Token Ring to the status of a strategic product by incorporating it within Systems Application Architecture (SAA). It has also increased its applicability by producing links between Token Ring and System 36 and 370 architecture computers.

See also: Lan (page 58).

UNIX

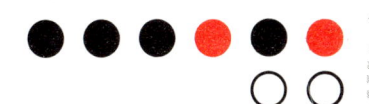

Unix is a multiuser operating system which is slowly becoming accepted as a *"de facto"* standard for all types of computer. Its major selling point is portability. Unix is written in a high-level language (C), and consequently can be run on almost any computer. Most operating systems are written in low-level languages and thus will run efficiently only on the machine they were designed for.

Unix is now offered by all the major mainframe and minicomputer manufacturers, and is available on everything from the smallest multiuser micro to the largest mainframe.

Portability is a popular feature with software developers, as it minimises the effort needed to adapt a system for use on a new computer. Unix also appeals to the technical cognoscenti because of its structure.

Unix is divided into a compact central kernel, plus a set of utilities that interact with it. This modular structure makes Unix easier to understand and to work with than most operating systems, and also increases reliability.

The kernel looks after the system filestore, provides protection and security arrangements, and allocates time and memory to user applications.

The most important of the utilities is known as the "shell", and sits between the user's terminal and the kernel. The shell implements the user's instructions by passing the appropriate system calls to the shell.

Unix has been widely criticised for its lack of user-friendliness, but this alleged failing is a characteristic of AT&T's version of Unix rather than inherent to the operating system itself. It is quite possible to write a different shell which provides the amount of user-friendliness desired.

One company which has done this is Microsoft, and its version of Unix, known as Xenix, has proved particularly popular.

Other variants of Unix similarly differ in the utilities they provide.

The proliferation of different versions of Unix has caused concern. Applications programs need to be tailored to suit each individual variant, and this destroys some of the advantage offered by the operating system's portability.

To overcome this problem, the Institute of Electrical and Electronics Engineers (IEEE) has developed a standard known as Posix, published in August 1988. Posix is a standardised form not of Unix itself, but of that part of it which sits between the kernel and the outside world.

Any application program which is compatible with Posix will be able to run under all versions of Unix which are themselves Posix-compatible.

It seems likely that the many different versions of Unix will eventually be reduced to two. One will be the AT&T version; the other will be developed by the Open Software Foundation, an organisation formed in 1988 by a group of companies, including IBM and DEC, to challenge AT&T's control of Unix. The Foundation is developing a new version of Unix based on IBM's AIX.

Unix emerged in 1971 from Bell Labs, the research subsidiary of AT&T. It was designed as a multiuser timesharing operating system for scientists working with DEC minicomputers.

AT&T was at the time prohibited by American antitrust legislation from competing in the computer market, so Unix was originally restricted to academic environments. The first copy arrived in the UK in 1974, but the first commercial version (System III) did not appear until 1980. This was superseded three years later by the present version, System V.

VANS

Value-added network services (Vans) comprise any service which uses a network and provides some facility additional to the network infrastructure.

This extra facility is normally some kind of software or data. Probably the earliest type of Vans, and certainly the largest today in terms of market revenues, is remote information retrieval; the added value is the specialist information of the database.

Other well-established types of Vans include videotex services such as British Telecom's Prestel and Istel's Infotrac. Here the added value is the presentation and access software: management facilities such as accounting information; and, with Prestel, the availability again of an information database.

Electronic mail services such as Telecom Gold and One-to-One are also Vans. So are electronic data interchange (EDI) services.

In 1986, the Department of Trade and Industry announced a market stimulation project known as Vanguard. This is designed to increase user awareness of the potential of applications-specific Vans such as EDI services, and to establish areas where they can be most useful.

Although Vans have been in existence for many years, the term came into use only in 1981, as a consequence of the deregulation of British Telecom. In that year the Government defined the terms under which Vans could operate in the new environment, and established a licensing procedure.

These regulations have since been revised following the first experiences of the deregulated market and in response to pressure from interested parties, mainly with a view to reducing British Telecom's power to dominate. The latest regulations were issued in autumn 1986.

See also: EDI (page 34).

VDU STANDARDS

A number of VDU standards for personal computers have come into use over the past few years, referred to by sets of initials such as CGA, EGA and VGA. The majority were formulated by IBM, and they represent a progression from the simple to the complex as the technology has developed and as new PC applications such as desktop publishing and computer-aided design have emerged.

The starting point is two standards introduced with the original IBM PC in 1981. MDA (Monochrome Display Adaptor) is for monochrome text only, and provides for characters to be constructed from a 9x14 matrix of dots.

CGA (Colour Graphics Adaptor) provides for both text and graphics. In text mode characters are constructed from an 8x8 matrix, lower resolution than that catered for by MDA. Colour graphics (with up to four colours) can be displayed in a screen format of 320 x 200 pixels. CGA also allows monochrome graphics with higher resolution, 640 x 200.

CGA screens provide unattractively low resolution of both text and graphics. To overcome this deficiency an American company called Hercules introduced its own Monochrome Display Adaptor (usually called a Hercules card), providing the same high text resolution as IBM's MDA and also offering monochrome graphics at better resolution than CGA, 720 x 348.

IBM responded by introducing EGA (Enhanced Graphics Adaptor) to improve its colour displays to the standard of Hercules' mono display.

EGA provides for higher-resolution characters, constructed from an 8x14 matrix, and three graphics modes: medium (four colours, 320 x 200 pixels), high (16 colours, 640 x 200) and ultra high (640 x 350), the last intended for applications such as computer-aided design and desktop publishing.

Each of these facilities was provided on the PC range via plug-in cards. When PS/2 was announced in 1987 IBM adopted a different policy, providing graphics display facilities via chips incorporated in the processor.

Two new standards were introduced. The first, MCGA (Multi Colour Graphics Array) is offered only on the entry-level Model 30 (and variants such as the Model 25). It provides for characters to be constructed from a 16x8 matrix, and two graphics modes: medium (256 colours or 64 grey shades, 320 x 200 pixels) and high (two colours or two grey shades, 640 x 480).

The other new standard is VGA (Video Graphics Array), offered on the four top models in the PS/2 range, the 50, 60, 70 and 80. It supports programs written in MDA, CGA or EGA. The character size is 9x16 dots, and there are two graphics modes: medium as in MCGA, and high (16 colours, 680 x 480 pixels).

VECTOR PROCESSING

Some computer-intensive applications take many hours of CPU time. Any way of reducing this time is desirable.

General-purpose computers are provided with instruction sets designed to permit arithmetic of a type known as scalar. This is conventional arithmetic of the type we are all familiar with. In technical language, an instruction operates on a pair of operands to produce a result. In a simple example, the instruction is "add", the operands are 1 and 2, and the result is 3.

Many large computational programs lend themselves to a different type of arithmetic, known as vector processing. Here the instruction operates on multiple pairs of operands to produce multiple results.

You could, for example, use vector processing to subtract tax from gross pay to realise the net pay for each member of an entire workforce. Here the number of pairs of operands, and the number of results, would be equal to the number of people in the workforce. It is the complete set of pairs of operands that is referred to as a vector.

In practice, commercial data processing applications such as payroll do not lend themselves to the vector processing technique. Scientific workloads, however, typically have 30% to 70% vectorisable content – that is, 30% to 70% of the total data can be arranged in the form of vectors.

You can use the vector processing technique to reduce the run time in two ways. First, you could process all the sums making up the vector in parallel, thus reducing the run time for the entire vector processing operation to that of a single scalar processing operation.

This is the technique used in array processors, such as the ICL Distributed Array Processor (DAP), offered as a peripheral with Series 39 mainframes.

The alternative technique, which is used by most vector processors, is known as pipelining. Here the process of fetching the operands for the next calculation is done at the same time as calculating the results of the first sum.

While this overlapping technique does not produce the same speed increase as array processing, it still provides very significant gains. How much depends on the nature of the application. A typical vector processing application will run two or three times as fast on a vector processor as it will on a scalar processor, and, for tasks that take several hours in total, this is clearly a worthwhile gain.

Companies with computing workloads that have a high degree of vectorisability can buy computers designed specifically for vector processing. These machines are usually called super-computers, and Cray Research is the market leader.

For companies with a mixed workload that would benefit from some degree of vector processing, the option is to buy a vector processor as an add-on to an existing mainframe. Most users of large mainframes are in this position, and consequently most mainframe manufacturers include an add-on vector processor in their catalogues.

IBM gave this approach respectability when it announced the VPF (Vector Processing Facility) for the 3090 mainframe series in October 1985. Most other manufacturers offer a similar product as an option: Honeywell Bull uniquely offers one as a standard integral component of its DPS 90 mainframe range.

Applications that lend themselves to vectorisation are those that are compute-intensive (rather than I/O-intensive), have large vectors, have limited conditional processing and take a lot of cpu time. Examples are engineering calculations (especially finite element analysis problems) financial modelling, and vehicle scheduling.

Fortran is the standard programming language for vector processing applications.

See also: Parallel processing (page 90).

VERTICAL RECORDING

Vertical recording is a new technique for recording data on magnetic media, especially discs.

Disc drive manufacturers are facing a serious problem. The rate of growth in demand for disc storage has been outstripping the rate of technical progress for several years. The time is looming when large computer systems will be unable to support the disc capacity their users need.

Vertical recording promises a quantum leap in packing density, possibly by as much as an order of magnitude. This would allow, for example, an increase in big mainframe disc spindle capacity from the current maximum of 3.75Gb to about 40Gb.

If available today, this capacity would satisfy projected user requirements for at least another five years.

Vertical recording has therefore attracted a lot of attention since the concept was first advanced in 1975, and the major disc manufacturers are all exploring its possibilities.

As with many other good ideas, theory is not always the same as practice. For a start, conventional recording media are not adequate for vertical recording: they are unable to store bits of the very small size required (at least 100,000 to the inch, compared with the 15,000 per inch maximum achieved today). So new recording media will be required, doubling the technical risk.

Read-write heads with smaller dimensions will also be needed, and there are other more esoteric technical problems to be solved. This means we are unlikely to see discs using vertical recording techniques much before the end of the decade.

The term "vertical recording" relates to the orientation of the magnetic domains representing bits within the recording medium.

On all existing disc drives, bits are stored horizontally: if you could look down on a disc and see them, they would appear like concentric circles of jelly beans laid end to end.

With vertical recording, the beans are rotated through 90° so as to stand side by side, and you would see only their tops.

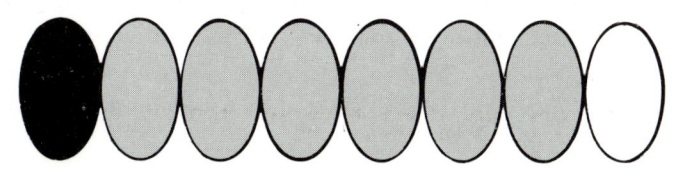

VIDEOTEX

A videotex system is a special type of computer system, designed to allow people with no experience of computers to access computer power, and particularly information bases, economically and without difficulty.

To achieve this there is a standardised, menu-driven user interface, and a standardised method of communication between terminals and central processor.

The combination of ease of use, standardised transmission protocols and low-cost terminals has made videotex very attractive in specialised application areas such as travel agencies and insurance brokers.

Over the past few years, videotex systems have come to be used in a much broader spectrum.

Generalising, applications that lend themselves to videotex tend to require communication with staff unfamiliar with computers; communication with many different users; a display of only a small amount of information at any one time; an information base that can be split into a hierarchy of up to five levels: and an information base that is of high value to the user.

Strictly speaking, there are no fewer than five different videotex standards. The one most widely used in this country is British Telecom's Prestel standard, and use of the word "videotex" in the UK nearly always means compatible with Prestel.

France, the US, Canada and Japan also have their own videotex standards. Outside these four countries, however, they are rarely met, whereas the Prestel standard is in use in about a dozen other countries outside the UK.

When it was publicly launched by British Telecom in 1979, Prestel consisted of a central system built round a database, and supporting a terminal network of users.

The terminals used were modified domestic televisions; user access was via a hand-held keypad similar to that used on teletext televisions; and transmission was performed using the telephone network.

Since then this principle has been modified. Purpose-built terminals with full alphanumeric keyboards have been introduced, allowing much greater interaction. Private videotex systems frequently use dedicated lines rather than the PSTN.

The term "viewdata" is sometimes used as a synonym for videotex. The standards-making body CCITT, however, has specified that videotex is the correct term.

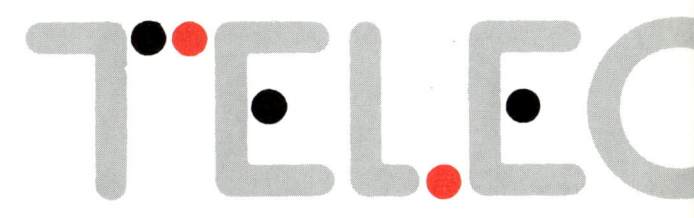

VLSI

VLSI stands for Very Large Scale Integration. It describes the basic technology from which both logic circuits and memory circuits are constructed in today's fourth generation computer systems.

That technology has developed over 25 years. It was in the early sixties that techniques were first evolved for integrating a number of electronic components such as capacitors, resistors and transistors into a complete electrical circuit made from a single piece of semiconducting material.

At that time the technology was known as LSI. Examples of computers which first embodied this technology, for logic circuits only, are the IBM 360 series and the ICL 1900 series.

As time went on the degree of integration became greater and greater: that is, the number of circuits that could be fabricated on a single piece of material ("a chip") became larger and larger. After a while, the term LSl seemed no longer adequate to describe the technology, and VLSI was adopted instead.

It was not until 1970 that LSI techniques were used to fabricate the main memories of computers: the pioneer was IBM with the 370/135 and 145. Within two or three years, every one of IBM's competitors had followed suit, and the predecessor ferrite core and plated wire memories disappeared.

This development, along with a number of others, led to the coinage of the term "fourth generation", though, as with the term "VLSI", it was adopted only gradually and there is no clear-cut dividing line.

The degree of integration of logic circuits is usually measured in terms of the number of gates (a gate being a device that implements a logic function). The maximum density today is 256K gates.

With memory circuits integration is measured in terms of the number of bits per chip. The maximum density today is one megabit per chip (128K bytes).

See also: Mainframe generations (page 65).

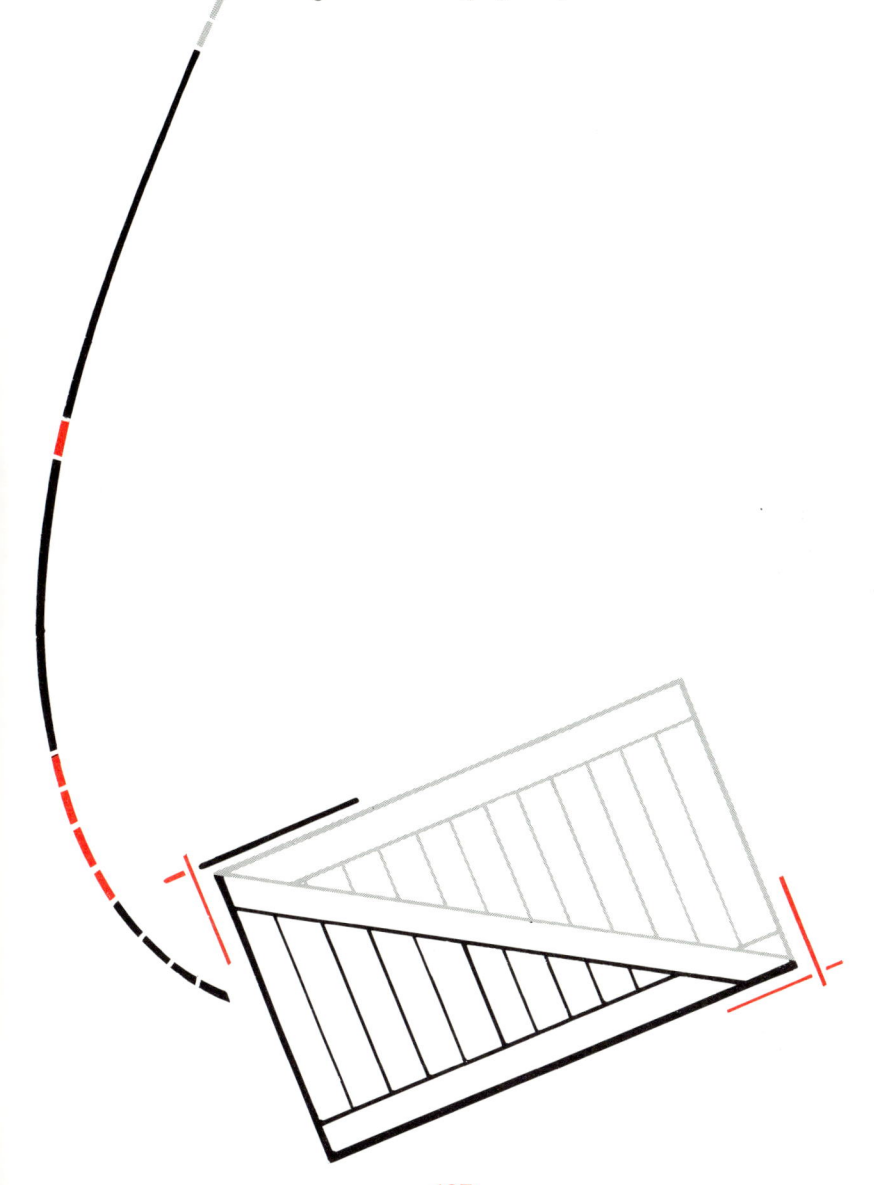

VON NEUMANN ARCHITECTURE

Virtually all computers ever built have conformed to an overall design pattern known as von Neumann architecture. It acquired this name from a seminal paper describing the architecture, published in the forties by a group of researchers headed by John von Neumann.

A major feature of this paper was that it recognised, and described, how programs could be treated in the same way as data (rather than requiring separate circuitry and storage). This was a major breakthrough, as it pointed the way to the concept of the stored alterable program computer. (Early computers such as Eniac had the program designed in, and thus were unalterable without a major engineering change.)

The von Neumann architecture has proved immensely satisfactory, and has reigned virtually without challenge for the first 40 years of computer history. Now however its limitations have started to become apparent, and the possibility of other architectures is being considered.

One major characteristic of von Neumann architecture is sequential operation: a program consists of a series of operations which must be performed in the same sequence each time. This applies to both data processing and scientific computing.

There are theoretically major gains to be made if you remove the need for sequential operation and process various elements of the same task in parallel. Parallel processing is the subject of much current research, and is one of the major elements of the fifth generation programme.

Moving from serial to parallel processing is however by no means a trivial change, and involves radical changes in software as well as hardware. For this reason, and because virtually no software exists today, it is certain that von Neumann computers will dominate computing until well into the next century.

Within the overall class of von Neumann machines, there are several subdivisions: special types of computer designed to achieve particular tasks more efficiently than a general-purpose system can do.

For computational work, there are specialist systems called array processors and vector processors, both designed to speed up mathematical calculations.

To boost reliability, many companies offer fault-tolerant systems. The principle here is that every system element is duplicated, so that in the event of any failure the back-up unit automatically takes over.

To boost performance, the concept of the reduced instruction set computer (Risc) has evolved. Here the size of the instruction set is reduced to allow each instruction to be executed more quickly.

See also: Mainframe generations (page 65).

WAFER SCALE INTEGRATION

Silicon chips are fabricated in batches of hundreds at a time on wafers. After fabrication the wafers are sawn up to create the individual chips, which are then packaged and mounted on printed circuit boards (PCBs).

To create a computer system, a number of chips have to be connected together. Chips on the same PCB are connected by metal tracks; the number of possible interconnections between chips is limited by the number of pins on the chip package.

The traditional way of increasing the power of computer systems has been to make the individual circuit components smaller, so that more of them can be packaged on a single chip, and so that the tracks connecting the components are shorter (and thus the time taken to transmit messages between components is less).

A potential alternative way of achieving an increase in power would be to manufacture all the chips required by a system on the same wafer. This would not only eliminate one stage in the manufacturing process, but would also allow speedier communication between chips and more connections between them.

This idea – the integration of some or all of the chips used in a computer processor or memory on a single wafer – is known as wafer scale integration (WSI).

The potential was first realised as soon as LSI devices were successfully manufactured. Texas Instruments tried to build a WSI logic device as early as 1967. It failed due to the low yield per wafer.

Failures of components on a wafer occur because the silicon it is made from has imperfections in it. When the wafer is due to be cut up into individual chips, this does not matter: the flawed components are thrown away, and the overall yield is high enough to make the process cost effective.

When the chips are linked together on the wafer, however, the yield is more critical. The larger the size of each component, the greater the chance it will be flawed. In those early days, the percentage of duff chips on each wafer was too high. Since then, improvements in the silicon manufacturing process coupled with greater miniaturisation have made wafer scale integration economic.

This led Gene Amdahl to conceive the idea of manufacturing an IBM-compatible mainframe out of WSI circuitry. It would have taken about 30 wafers, each containing between one and two million components, to have made each processor.

Amdahl established a company called Trilogy to design and manufacture the machine. Such was his reputation that he attracted funding variously estimated at between $200 and $400 million, and the support of computer companies including Bull, DEC and Sperry.

Trilogy was formed in 1981, and struggled for three years to implement Amdahl's ambitious plans before finally admitting defeat in August 1984. Amdahl has since argued that his effort proved that WSI was possible, but was not economic because of advances in VLSI chip design.

Others however have argued that Trilogy's failure was due to its attempt to use high-speed ECL technology to build the wafers. ECL circuitry needs a lot of power, which creates heat dissipation problems.

Trilogy also suffered from the problem that besets every WSI designer, that of ensuring that the faulty chips are bypassed. The Trilogy solution was to triplicate each chip, which necessarily increased by a factor of three the space needed to carry out a given amount of functionality.

Since the Trilogy failure, WSI techniques have been used to fabricate Mos memories (as opposed to ECL logic) with rather more success. Prototype devices have been shown at a number of conferences, though no one has yet succeeded in entering commercial production.

One company attempting to do so is Anamartic, founded in 1986 to carry out WSI development work initiated at Sinclair Research's Metalab research centre in 1983.

There are three important differences between the Trilogy and Anamartic projects. Anamartic is attempting to build a memory rather than a processor; it is using Nmos technology rather than ECL: and it is using soft chip connections rather than hard wiring.

Anamartic's device is intended to be an intermediate speed memory device, slower and cheaper than Ram, but about 1000 times faster than disc drives.

This low speed requirement allows Anamartic to use Nmos technology, which has low power consumption, and thus eliminates the heat dissipation problems experienced by Trilogy.

In solving the chip interconnection problem with software, Anamartic is drawing on the work of Ivor Catt, a British scientist who patented his ideas in 1970, but could not get commercial backing to develop them until Sinclair took up the idea in 1983. Anamartic has now bought Catt's patents.

The Alvey project also recognised the potential of WSI, and allocated £2.5 million towards a research project being led by Plessey, aimed at finding a method of designing WSI circuits with effective fault tolerance.

The project aims to develop a method of designing redundancy so as to allow soft reconfiguration, so that defective circuits can be bypassed using software control on the wafer. The idea is that this facility should be used both when testing wafers in the factory and in the field each time a system incorporating the wafer is powered up.

WORKSTATION

A decade ago, workstations did not exist. We had computers and we had terminals. As the cost of computer logic came down, it became possible to manufacture terminals with memories and disc drives at economic cost. It also became possible to produce low-cost computers for individual use. Thus were born the intelligent terminal and the personal computer.

Originally, the two devices were used for quite different tasks. An intelligent terminal was used purely for online work, a personal computer for standalone processing. But as people came to appreciate the potential of both devices, so the boundary line between them became blurred.

Terminals were used more and more for processing in their own right, while PCs were hooked up to mainframes. They were also linked in networks, so as to be able to interchange data and share expensive resources such as printers.

These new circumstances led to the creation of the new term. A workstation was a processing device used by individuals as an essential part of their work, and which was connected to a larger system and/or network.

The fall in technology prices made possible at the same time systems capable of processing applications such as computer-aided design and engineering. Previously, these applications could be run cost-effectively only on mainframes or large minis.

Now however manufacturing companies can purchase very powerful systems with high-resolution graphics screens and processing power measured in mips, at prices which justify their use by individual designers and engineers.

These systems started to appear in volume around 1985, and their use has dramatically boosted the computer-aided design market. The most successful companies in this area have been start-ups Apollo and Sun.

These systems are most cost-effective when used on a network, and are invariably supplied with powerful communications capabilities. The term workstation was adopted for use with these devices too, and is today most commonly used in this context.

See also: Cim (page 13).

X.25

X.25 is a protocol defining the message structure required by terminals and computers connected to packet-switching networks. It was formulated by the Consultative Committee for International Telephony and Telegraphy (CCITT), the representative body of the PTTs and common carriers, and adopted as a recommendation in 1976.

X.25 defines three levels of protocol – the physical layer, the link layer, and the network, or packet, layer. These conform to the lowest three levels of the ISO model for Open Systems Interconnection.

X.25 was designed for use on public data communications networks, and is used, for example, by British Telecom on PSS. It is also used for private wide area networks, especially those which are designed to link with PSS or its international counterpart, IPSS.

The term packet-switching itself requires some explanation. When data communications originally evolved, the transmission medium chosen was the telephone network. This is circuit-switched – that is, there is a physical transmission path (the circuit) connecting the two communicating devices.

Circuit-switching is inefficient, as the circuit is completely tied up for the whole period that the transmission is taking place. So when data comms traffic grew to the extent that the PTTs saw a market in dedicated digital data comms networks, thought was given to the question of improving efficient use.

This led to the evolution of packet-switching, a technique whereby a message is broken down into small units or packets.

Each packet is created with control information including the destination address, and is sent independently of its fellow packets through the network to the destination. At this point the packets are reassembled into the original message.

Naturally, there has to be a standardised way of doing this.

CCITT has produced a whole series of X-series standards (the "X" indicates digital). X.25 is the most important of these, and is often therefore used as a synonym for packet-switching, or for public packet-switching networks.

See also: OSI (page 89).

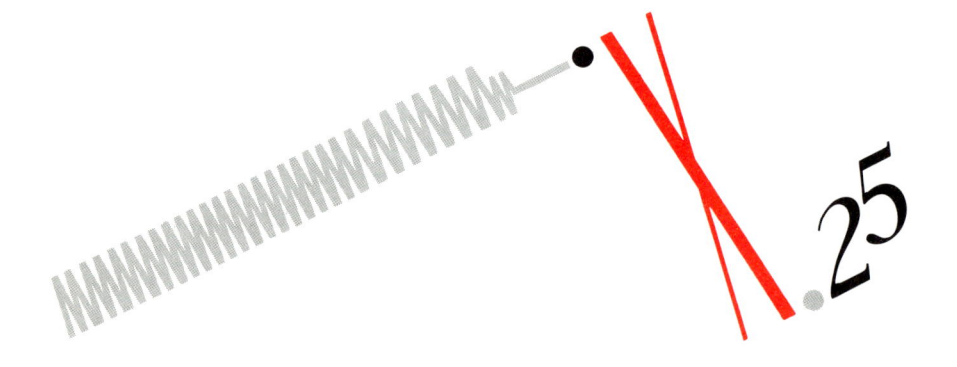

X.400

Organisations that wish to adopt electronic mail have a variety of choices. They can use a publicly available service such as Telecom Gold, Easylink, One-to-One or Quikcomm. If they already have a computer network, they can provide e-mail facilities for all its users by acquiring a software package from the manufacturer.

The trouble with all these options is that the number of people that can be reached through each of them is severely limited. None of them is compatible, so accessing an alien service requires a gateway, and it is impractical to have gateways to all the alternatives.

As a result, telex is still the most widely used e-mail service, despite its many shortcomings. There are 115,000 telex terminals in use in the UK, and about two million worldwide.

The establishment of a set of e-mail international standards is thus highly desirable. CCITT, the representative body of the world's national post and telecomms authorities, has addressed itself to this requirement, and the outcome is a set of standards known as X.400.

X.400 specifies the procedures involved in setting up a comprehensive message-handling service, covering such essentials as methods of addressing and routing. It also specifies methods of inter-communication between telex, teletex and fax services.

Software house Sydney Development Corp became the first company to announce a commercially available X.400 system in 1986, when it introduced Messenger 400. British Telecom introduced its Message Handling Service implementing X.400 in 1987.

See also: OSI (page 89), Teletex (page 110).

X-Stream

X-Stream is a range of data communications services introduced by British Telecom during the eighties. The common element is digital transmission, used in place of the analogue transmission found on the telephone network and Datel private circuits ("X" is the international symbol for digital operation).

There are four X-Stream services. The first, PSS (Packet Switchstream), is a public network offering an alternative to the telephone network (PSTN). The digital transmission techniques give the user three major benefits.

First, PSS has higher performance – currently 48K bits per second (48Kbps) compared with the maximum 9.6Kbps on the PSTN. Second, you don't need to convert your digital data into analogue form and back again, and so you don't need modems. Third, the line quality on PSS is higher, so the error rate is lower.

The other major difference between PSS and the PSTN is that PSS is packet-switched and the PSTN circuit-switched. Packet-switching makes for more efficient network utilisation, and therefore (theoretically at least) for lower charges to the customer.

These are the intrinsic advantages of PSS. British Telecom has compounded them by devising a tariff structure which allows you to pay for all transmissions at local call rates.

For users PSS is more cost-effective than the phone network for large-scale usage, such as high-volume transaction-processing applications. In the long term, it is likely to replace the PSTN for nearly all purely data communications traffic.

The other three X-Stream services all offer private digital services, and are alternatives to the existing range of Datel circuits. The major benefits are the same as those offered to public network users by PSS.

Private circuits are constructed from individual lines between the two offices to be linked and their local exchanges. For digital circuits, the exchanges have to be digital (such as System X) and so does the transmission medium connecting the exchanges.

This transmission medium has traditionally been the trunk line element of the PSTN. It was not until a substantial part of the trunk network had been converted to digital operation that private digital circuits could be introduced. This took place in January 1982, five months after the commercial launch of PSS.

The first two X-Stream private circuits are known as Kilostream and Megastream. Kilostream offers circuits ranging from 2.4Kbps to 64Kbps, roughly the same speed range as the existing Datel private circuits.

Megastream operates at much higher speed – at present 2Mbps or 8Mbps. Megastream circuits are therefore suitable for high-volume data transmission users with very large private networks, such as banks and building societies.

The third X-Stream service, Satstream, was introduced a couple of years later in 1984. It differs from Kilostream and Megastream in that satellites are used as the transmission medium rather than the trunk network. This is valuable for wide-area private circuits, and also in locations remote from urban centres such as oil rigs. The speed range is 41Kbps to 1,920 Kbps.

APPENDIX 1

ABBREVIATIONS OF TECHNICAL TERMS

This appendix explains all abbreviations of technical terms used in the text (except those relating to proprietary products), plus some others which are commonly encountered. Where there is a more detailed explanation in the text, the place to look is indicated.

ADP   Automatic Data Processing
Term used before the invention of the computer to describe electromechanical systems used for automating the administration of commercial procedures

AI   Artificial Intelligence
Discipline which attempts to make machines display human qualities, especially in reasoning and in forming judgments
[see under Artificial intelligence]

APL   A Programming Language
Programming language favoured by theorists, but used only by a small minority of computer installations

Apse   Ada Project Support Environment
Set of systems design tools used to support development of systems written in the Ada programming language
[see under Ada]

ASCII   American Standard Code for Information Interchange
A widely accepted standard method for coding data within computers

Asic   Application Specific Integrated Circuit
Logic chip customised to perform a specific function

ATM   Automated Teller Machine
On-line cash dispenser

Basic   Beginners' All-Purpose Symbolic Instruction Code
Programming language used particularly on microcomputers

BIOS   Basic Input Output System
Part of an operating system which handles processing of inputs and outputs

bps   Bits Per Second
Measure of data transmission speed

Cad   Computer-Aided Design (or Computer-Aided Drafting)
Type of computer system used by engineers to assist task of product design
[see under Cim]

Cad/cam   Computer-Aided Design/Computer-Aided Manufacture
A Cad system which is additionally capable of producing outputs which can be used to control the operation of machine tools
[see under Cim]

Cais   Common Apse Interface Set
Ipse promoted by US Government for use with Ada design projects
[see under Ada]

Case   Computer-Aided Software Engineering
Use of computer technology to assist applications development within a framework specified by a design methodology
[see under Case]

CD-Rom   Compact Disc-Read Only Memory
Optical disc supplied with pre-recorded information that cannot be changed by the user
[see under Optical disc]

CGA   Colour Graphics Adaptor
IBM standard specifying a certain quality of VDU resolution
[see under VDU standards]

Cim Computer Integrated Manufacturing
Concept of integrating all the different computer systems used to control or assist in the manufacturing process
[see under Cim]

Cmos Complementary Metal Oxide Semiconductor
Technology most commonly used to construct logic for small computer systems
[see under Cmos/ECL]

CNC Computer Numerical Control
Technique for controlling operation of machine tools with tapes created by a computer system
[see under Cim]

Cobol Common Business Oriented Language
Most widely used programming language; designed for data processing applications

Com Computer Output to Microfilm/Microform/Microfiche
Peripheral equipment used to record computer data on film for archival purposes

cps Characters Per Second
Measure of data transfer speed within a computer system

CPU Central Processing Unit
Part of the computer where programs are executed

CRT Cathode Ray Tube
The technology used to construct most VDUs: commonly used as a synonym for VDU, particularly in the US

CSMA Carrier Sense Multiple Access
Protocol used to transmit messages on an Ethernet Lan
[see under Token ring]

CUG Closed User Group
Collection of people alone authorised to use a particular system on a network

DASD Direct Access Storage Device
Magnetic disc drive where disc is permanently on-line; term used mainly for discs on large mainframes

DBMS Database Management System
Software product used to create and access a structured collection of data
[see under Database]

DCA Document Content Architecture
IBM protocol used to code documents for transmission between systems
[see under ODA]

DDBMS Distributed Database Management System
A database management system which allows access to more than one database at the same time
[see under Distributed database]

DDL Data Description Language
Special-purpose programming language used to specify the structure of a database
[see under Database]

DIA Document Interchange Architecture
IBM protocol used for transmitting documents between systems

DML Data Manipulation Language
Special-purpose programming language used to describe the operations to be performed on a database by an applications program
[see under Database]

DP Data Processing
Collective term for commercial computer applications (as opposed to scientific), they are characterised by large amounts of data manipulation and small amounts of computation – examples are invoicing, payroll and stock control

DPM Data Processing Manager
The most common term for the executive responsible for an organisation's computing activities

Dram Dynamic Random Access Memory
Type of chip used in most computers' main memory
[see under Cycle time]

DTP Desk Top Publishing
Technique for using personal computers to produce printed output of a quality comparable to that found in books
[see under Desktop publishing]

EBCDIC Extended Binary-Coded Decimal Interchange Code
A standard method for coding data within computers

ECL Emitter-Coupled Logic
Technology most commonly used to construct logic for powerful computer systems
[see under Cmos/ECL]

EDI Electronic Data Interchange
Technique for exchanging business transaction data
[see under Electronic data interchange]

Edifact EDI For Administration, Commerce and Transport
Set of standardised syntax rules for EDI
[see under Electronic data interchange].

EDP Electronic Data Processing
Data processing by computer

EFT Electronic Funds Transfer
Technique for exchanging financial transaction data

EGA Enhanced Graphics Adaptor
IBM standard specifying a certain quality of VDU resolution
[see under VDU standards]

Eprom Erasable Programmable Read-Only Memory
Type of memory chip that cannot be written to while installed in a computer, but can be written to initially using special equipment, and can then be reprogrammed using the same equipment as circumstances change

Esprit European Strategic Programme for Research in IT
Fifth generation research project organised by the EEC
[see under Esprit]

flops Floating Point Operations Per Second
Measure of performance of computers used in scientific applications

Fortran FORmula TRANslation Programming language favoured for scientific applications

GaAs Gallium Arsenide
Technology used to construct logic circuits for certain types of computer
[see under Gallium arsenide]

Gb Gigabyte
Unit of measure of computer memory capacity; equals 2 to the power of 30 (roughly equal to one billion) bytes (characters) of data

GCR Group Coded Recording
IBM-pioneered method of recording data on magnetic tape which provides very high recording density

HDA Head Disc Assembly
Sealed component of a Winchester disc drive incorporating the disc platters and the read/write heads

IC Integrated Circuit
Basic component of third and fourth generation computer systems

IDA Integrated Digital Access
ISDN service run by British Telecom
[see under ISDN]

I/O Input/Output
The procedures or systems used to feed data into a computer and to produce data from it

ips Inches Per Second
Measure of magnetic tape system performance

Ipse Integrated Project Support Environment
An integrated set of systems development tools covering the specification, design, programming, building and testing of computer systems
[see under Ipse]

IPSS International Packet-Switched Service
Public international data communications service run by British Telecom

IRDS Information Resource Dictionary System
ANSI standard for data dictionaries
[see under Data dictionary]

ISDN Integrated Services Digital Network
Combined voice and data communications service for which standards are currently being formulated by CCITT
[see under ISDN]

IT Information Technology
Computer-based equipment, including computers, word processors, process control systems and communications equipment

Kb Kilobyte
Unit of measure of computer memory capacity; equals 1,024 (2 to the power of 10) bytes (characters) of data

Lan Local Area Network
An interconnected group of personal computers or workstations
[see under Lan]

Lips Logical Inferences Per Second
Measure of performance of fifth generation computers which process data using artificial intelligence techniques

LSI Large Scale Integration
Technology used in computers which integrates a large number of electronic components in a single piece of semiconducting material
[see under VLSI]

Map Manufacturing Applications Protocol
Set of standards within OSI framework designed for manufacturing applications
[see under Map/Top]

Mb Megabyte
Unit of measure of computer memory capacity; equals 2 to the power of 20 (roughly equal to one million) bytes (characters) of data

MCA Micro Channel Architecture
IBM architecture designed for its PS/2 personal computer range

MCGA Multi Colour Graphics Array
IBM standard specifying a certain quality of VDU resolution
[see under VDU standards]

MDA Monochrome Display Adaptor
IBM standard specifying a certain quality of VDU resolution
[see under VDU standards]

MHz MegaHertz
Measure of internal computer processor speed, used mainly for personal computers: indicates number of millions of clock cycles per second
[see under Cycle time]

mips Millions of Instructions Per Second
Measure of internal computer processor speed, used mainly for mainframes and minicomputers: indicates number of machine instructions executed per second
[see under Mips]

MIS Management Information System
Software suite which takes information from day-to-day applications and processes it to provide useful information for management

MMI Man-Machine Interface
The means by which a user interacts with a computer system

Mos Metal Oxide Semiconductor
One of the two major technologies used to construct both logic and memory circuits for computer systems (the other is bipolar)

MOTIS Message-Oriented Text Interchange System
Draft ISO standard designed to extend the facilities provided by the X.400 electronic mail standard

MTBF Mean Time Between Failure
Measure of reliability used with computer systems and their component parts

MTTR Mean Time to Repair
Measure of ease of repair used with computer systems and their component parts; used almost invariably in conjunction with MTBF

NC Numerical control
Technique for controlling operation of machine tools with pre-punched tapes
[see under Cim]

Nmos N-channel Metal Oxide Semiconductor
Type of Mos technology used for constructing elements of computer systems

OCR Optical Character Recognition
Technique for reading specially defined character fonts by machine

ODA Office Document Architecture
A developing set of international standards for transmitting documents between incompatible computer systems
[see under ODA]

OEM Original Equipment Manufacturer
Company that manufactures products which are sold to computer systems suppliers rather than end-users

OSI Open Systems Interconnection
Set of internationally agreed standards being formulated to allow incompatible computer systems to interwork with each other without the need for

intermediary translation devices
[see under OSI]

PABX Private Automatic Branch eXchange
Computer-based telephone exchange for an individual organisation or building

PAD Packet Assembly-Disassembly
Procedure executed at both ends of a packet-switched transmission, involving breaking down a message into packets at the transmitting end, and reassembling the message from its component packets at the receiving end

PC Personal Computer
Microprocessor-based computer system used by a single individual

PCB Printed Circuit Board
An element of a computer system, consisting of a number of chips and other electronic components mounted on a single board

PCM Plug-Compatible Manufacturer
A company that manufactures or supplies equipment which is completely compatible with the corresponding IBM equipment

PCTE Portable Common Tool Environment
An integrated project support environment developed under the Esprit fifth generation research project
[see under Ipse]

PGA Professional Graphics Adaptor
IBM standard specifying a certain quality of VDU resolution

PL/I Programming Language/One
Programming language created by IBM with the objective of combining the virtues of commercial and scientific languages

Pos Point Of Sale
Terminal equipment used in retail outlets to facilitate the job of cashiers while at the same time generating useful management information

POWU Post Office Work Unit
Standard benchmark used for measuring computer performance in the sixties and seventies, now obsolete

Prom Programmable Read-Only Memory
Type of memory chip that can be written to when received by the user using special equipment, but cannot thereafter be altered

PSS Packet SwitchStream
British Telecom data communications service which operates using packet-switching techniques
[see under X-Stream]

PSTN Public Switched Telephone Network
The telephone system run by British Telecom, when used as a data communications service; term used to contrast with other BT datacomms services such as PSS.

PTT Postal, Telegraph and Telephone agency
Generic term for organisations which run a national communications service

Race Research in Advanced Communications in Europe
Pan-European research programme instigated by the EEC
[see under Esprit]

Ram Random Access Memory
A computer's main memory; used mainly with personal computers to distinguish from Rom

RAS Reliability, Availability, Serviceability Term used to cover all the technical and service elements involved in ensuring computers run with as little disruption as possible

RDBMS Relational Data Base Management System
A type of database management system designed to make it easy for users to make ad hoc enquiries without needing programming skills
[see under Relational database]

Risc Reduced Instruction Set Computer

A type of computer designed to have high performance in applications characterised by a high volume of calculation
[see under Risc]

Rom Read-Only Memory
Type of memory which is supplied in a computer containing a program or data, and which cannot be altered by the user

SAA Systems Application Architecture
IBM proprietary set of procedures designed to standardise the way that programs interact with the outside world (including users, other programs and operating systems)
[see under SAA]

SNA Systems Network Architecture
IBM framework for constructing networks from IBM products
[see under SNA]

SQL Structured Query Language
Standardised high-level language used by programmers to write routines for querying relational databases
[see under SQL]

SSADM Structured Systems Analysis and Design Methodology
A set of structural and procedural standards designed by the UK Government for controlling large system developments
[see under Design methodologies]

TCM Thermal Conduction Module
Logic packaging technology used in large IBM systems

Top Technical Office Protocol
Set of standards within OSI framework designed for office applications
[see under Map/Top]

TTL Transistor-Transistor Logic
Bipolar technology used for constructing computer processors

Vans Value-Added Network Service
A service offered on a public network which provides some facility additional to the network infrastructure
[see under Vans]

VAR Value-Added Reseller
Company which buys a computer from a manufacturer and then adds facilities (usually software) before selling it to an end-user

VDU Visual Display Unit
Screen with input device such as keyboard or mouse used to display results of computer processing to user

VGA Video Graphics Array
IBM standard specifying a certain quality of VDU resolution
[see under VDU standards]

VLSI Very Large Scale Integration
Technology used in computers which integrates a very large number of electronic components in a single piece of semiconducting material
[see under VLSI]

VTAM Virtual Telecommunication Access Method
IBM software product used for controlling data communications between computer systems

Wan Wide Area Network
Network of computers linked by communications lines rather than by cables

Worm Write Once Read Many
Type of optical disc that can only be written to once by the user, and so is usually used for archival applications
[see under Optical disc]

WSI Wafer Scale Integration
Process of manufacturing a substantial number of the chips used in a computer processor or memory on the same wafer of silicon
[see under Wafer scale integration]

Wysiwyg What You See Is What You Get
Technique for displaying output on a VDU in exactly the same form and format that it will be printed

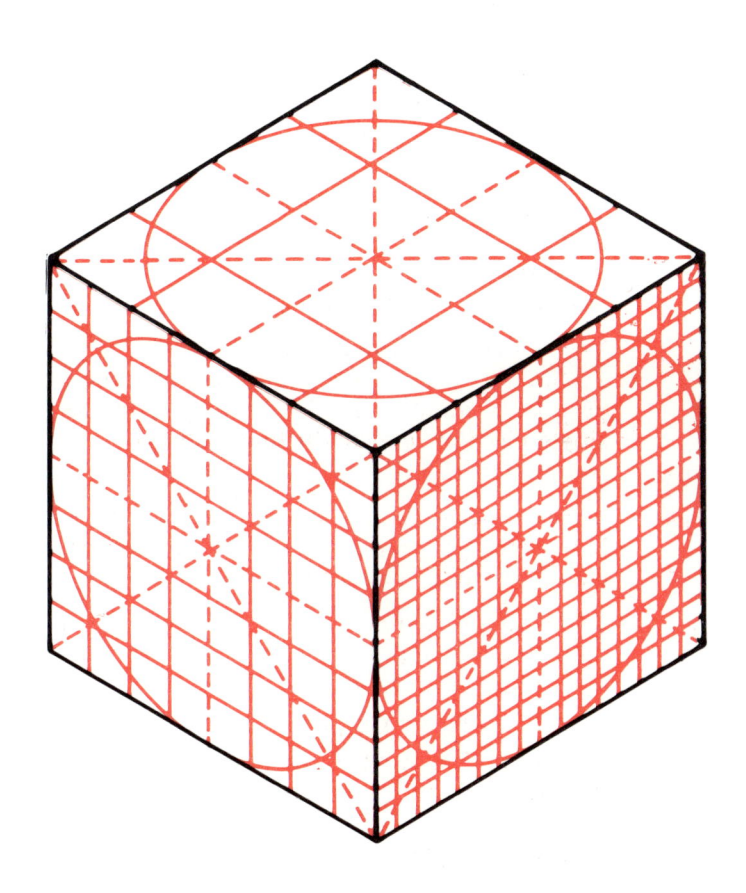

APPENDIX 2
ABBREVIATIONS OF ORGANISATIONS

This appendix explains all abbreviations of organisations used in the text (except those relating to computer systems and product vendors), plus some others which are commonly encountered. Where there is a detailed description of the organisation in the text, the place to look is indicated.

ACARD Advisory Council for Applied Research and Development
UK Government body which has produced a number of reports on the IT industry

ACM Association for Computer Machinery
US professional body roughly equivalent to the British Computer Society

ADAPSO Association of Data Processing Services Organisations
US trade association roughly equivalent to the Computing Services Association

AICS Association of Independent Computer Specialists
UK trade association of individuals who offer computer consultancy services

AJPO Ada Joint Programming Office
US Government body set up to ensure Ada programming language products conform to the standard specification

ANSI American National Standards Institute
US organisation concerned with formulating standards, which is particularly prominent in the area of programming languages

BCS British Computer Society
UK professional body for computer professionals

BEITA	Business Equipment and Information Technology Association UK trade association for suppliers
BMMG	British Microcomputer Manufacturers Group UK trade association and pressure group
BSI	British Standards Institution UK national body responsible for formulating standards in all areas of activity, including computing
CCITT	Comite Consultatif Internationale de Telegraphique et Telephonique Representative body of the world's public telecomms administrations, noted for its formulation of telecomms standards [see under CCITT]
CCTA	Central Computer and Telecommunications Agency UK Government body which coordinates the activities to Government computer departments.
CECUA	Confederation of European Computer User Associations Collective body for national associations of user groups
CEPT	Conference Europeennes des administrations des Postes et des Telecommunications Representative body of European public telecommunications administrations
Codasyl	COnference of DAta SYstems Languages Organisation which formulated standards for Cobol and for database management systems
COS	Corporation for Open Systems Group formed from computer equipment suppliers worldwide to promote the adoption of open systems
COSI	Computing Services Industry Training Council Body formed by the Computing Services Association to promote solutions to the skills shortage
CSA	Computing Services Association

Trade association for large services companies such as bureaux and systems houses

ECLAT European Computer Leasing and Trading Association
Trade association for computer leasing and broking companies

Ecma European Computer Manufacturers' Association
Representative body for European computer equipment suppliers which plays a major role in standards formulation

ECSA European Computing Services Association
European collective body of national computing services trade associations

Eurosinet EURopean Open Systems Interconnection NETwork
Pressure group formed by European computer equipment suppliers to promote development of OSI standards

FAST Federation Against Software Theft
UK pressure group formed to campaign for better protection of the rights of software developers

GUIDE Guidance for Users of Integrated Data processing Equipment
User group for users of IBM large systems worldwide

Idea International Data Exchange Association
Representative body of EDI service suppliers

IDPM Institute of Data Processing Management
UK professional body for computer professionals

IEE Institution of Electrical Engineers
UK professional body for electronic engineers

IEEE Institute of Electrical and Electronic Engineers
US professional body for electronic engineers; has formulated a number of important standards such as Ethernet and Posix

IFIP International Federation for Information Processing
Representative body of national professional societies, noted for its triennial congress

ISO	International Standards Organisation The senior standards-making body for all activities, including computing [see under ISO]
ITUSA	Information Technology Users Standards Association A UK user association formed to promote the development and adoption of standards
NCC	National Computing Centre Body formed by UK Government to promote the use of computing in the UK [see under NCC]
NCUF	National Computer Users Forum Collective body of UK user associations
Oftel	OFfice of TELecommunications Body appointed by UK Government to oversee operations of British Telecom after privatisation
OSF	Open Software Foundation Group of companies including DEC and IBM formed to develop a standardised form of Unix
Pitcom	Parliamentary Information Technology COMmittee Group of MPs formed to discuss information technology matters
SERC	Science Engineering Research Council Government body formed to promote Government policy in science and engineering; provides funding for information technology research projects involving both industry and academia
Sitpro	Simplification of International Trade PROcedures Board Body which has been instrumental in formulating guidelines for EDI services
SPAG	Standards Promotions and Applications Group Body formed from European computer equipment suppliers to promote the adoption of open systems
TEMA	Telecommunications Engineering and Manufactur-

ing Association
UK trade association for suppliers

TMA   Telecommunications Managers Association
UK representative body for managers of telecommunications installations

UKCMG   UK Computer Measurement Group
UK interest group for suppliers and users interested in computer performance matters

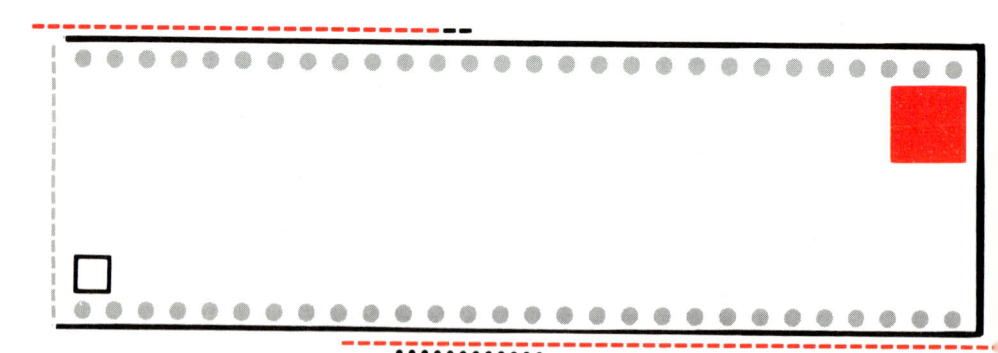

APPENDIX 3
UNITS OF MEASURE

Computer data, and the capacities of computer equipment processing, storing and transmitting that data, are described using three different units of measure: bit, byte and word.

Bit is a contraction of binary digit, and means a 0 or a 1. Information is represented within computers in binary form because a computer is in essence just a complex of switches. A switch which is off is taken to equal 0, a switch which is on equals 1.

Computers handle information which is other than purely numeric. This includes text characters, punctuation marks, mathematical symbols and so on. There is therefore a need to represent these non-numeric entities in terms of binary digits.

A variety of coding systems has been devised to achieve this end. One of the most widely used is the ASCII code, which allows you to express all digits and alphabetic characters plus a wide range of symbols in a code which can be encompassed within eight bits. For this reason, a unit of eight bits has become widely accepted as a useful size for the management of data within computer systems.

This unit is known as a byte, a term first coined by IBM. It has become standard practice to measure data capacities of computer memories in terms of the number of bytes.

Use of the byte alone as a management unit has its drawbacks, however. If a byte is used to represent a binary number (as opposed to a coded character), the maximum number that can be expressed is 11111111, which is 255 in decimal notation. Thus use of the byte as the only unit for storing data restricts your addressing ability to 255 locations. It also limits the complexity of the arithmetic you can do.

For this reason most computers are capable of managing data in larger units, which are usually (though not always) equal to an exact number of bytes. This larger unit is known as a word. Typical word lengths are 16 bits (two bytes) and 32 bits (four bytes), though much larger units are also found, particularly in systems used for large-scale computational problems.

Computers handle such large capacities of data that measurement in terms of bits, bytes and words is on its own inadequate. For example, a database for a typical large organisation today will total many billions of bytes. Numbers this large demand a new terminology.

The same type of problem is encountered when measuring computer speeds. The cycle time of a large computer – the time taken to change one set of switches on or off – is only a few billionths of a second: such a system will have anything up to 100 million cycles a second.

In practice, therefore, computer capacities and speeds are measured using compounds of words such as bit and second. These compounds are formed from SI units (Systeme Internationale d'unites) which are listed below.

1. Compounds for numbers greater than 1,000

Short number	Actual number	prefix	Symbol
2 to the power of 10	1,024	kilo	K
2 to the power of 20	1,048,576	mega	M
2 to the power of 30	1,073,741,824	giga	G
2 to the power of 40	1,099,511,627,776	tera	T

Strictly speaking, these prefixes were specified to mean exact multiples of 10 rather than 2: thus one megabyte should equal exactly one million bytes, and so on. Because the computer industry necessarily operates in multiples of two, the actual numbers listed above are more accurate.

2. Compounds for numbers that are a small fraction of 1

Short number	fraction of 1	prefix	Symbol
10 to the power of − 3	thousandth	milli	m
10 to the power of − 6	millionth	micro	mu
10 to the power of − 9	billionth	nano	n
10 to the power of − 12	trillionth	pico	p
10 to the power of − 15	thousand-trillionth	femto	

Today, switching speeds of even the fastest electronic circuits are "only" as low as a small number of picoseconds. The femto compound has not yet therefore come into widespread use, and there is no generally accepted symbol for it.

INDEX

Notes:

Numbers in bold indicate that the index term is the subject of the chapter found on that page or pages.

Names of products are excluded from the index, except in special cases such as Unix.

ACARD, 154
ACM, 154
Ada, **3–4**, 49, 52
ADAPSO, 154
ADP, 79, 140
Advanced Manufacturing Technology Centre, 15
AI (artificial intelligence), **7–8**, 39, 76, 140
AIC (Artificial Intelligence Corp), 8
AICS, 154
AJPO (Ada Joint Program Office), 4, 154
Albrecht, AJ, 48
Aldus Corp, 31
Algol, 3
Alliant, 91
Alvey, 44, 132
Amdahl Corp, 17, 18
Amdahl, Gene, 131
analyst workbench, **5–6**, 10
Anamartic, 131–2
ANSI, 25, 56, 105, 106, 154
APL, 3, 47, 140
Apollo, 133
APPC, 61
Apple Computer, 30
application generators, 46, 101
Applied Data Research, 32
Apse (Ada project support environment), 4, 52, 140

array processor, 91, 120, 121, 129
Arthur Young, 6
artificial intelligence (AI), **7–8**, 39, 76, 140
ASCII, 140, 159
Ashton-Tate, 47
Asic, 140
assembler language, 46, 48
AT&T, 11, 94, 99, 115, 116
ATM, 141

Babbage, Charles, 4, 82
Barclays Merchant Bank, 68
baseband, 38, 67
Basic, 3, 49, 75, 100, 141
BCS (British Computer Society), 154
Bednorz, Georg, 108
BEITA, 155
Bell Labs, 82, 116
benchmark, 70, 71
BIOS, 141
bipolar, 16, 50, 66, 148
BIS, 52
bit, 159
BMMG, 155
Boeing, 67
BP, 68
bps, 141
British Gas, 52
British Tab, 65

British Telecom (BT), 11, 34, 54, 55, 68, 69, 87, 88, 95, 110, 117, 124, 135, 137, 138–9
broadband, 37, 67
BSI (British Standards Institution), 56, 57, 105, 155
bubble memory, 16
Bull, 78, 131
Burroughs, 41, 65, 71
bus, 63, 91, 92
Butler Cox, 30
byte, 159

C (programming language), 101, 115
Cable & Wireless, 68
cache, 20
Cad (Computer-aided design/drafting), 5, 14, 118, 133, 141
Cad/Cam, 14, 141
Cais (Common Apse Interface Set), 4, 53, 141
Cambridge University, 108, 109
Case (Computer-aided software engineering) **9–10**, 24, 141
Catt, Ivor, 132
CCITT, **11–12**, 54, 55, 56, 78, 89, 110, 125, 135, 136, 137, 155
CCTA, 28, 155
CD-Rom, 86, 141
CECUA, 155
Ceefax, 111
CEPT, 155
CGA, 118, 119, 141
channel, 63
chess-playing computers, 8
Cim (Computer integrated manufacturing), **13–15**, 36, 142
Cincom, 22
circuit-switching, 135, 138
CMC, 93
Cmos, **16–17**, 66, 142
CNC, 13, 142
Cobol, 3, 22, 46, 48, 49, 75, 101, 142
Codasyl, 22, 155

Codd, Edgar, 32, 96, 97
Com, 142
communications server, 45
Computer-aided design/drafting (Cad), 5, 14, 118, 133, 141
computer-aided engineering, 133
computer-aided software engineering (Case), **9–10**, 24, 141
Computer integrated manufacturing (Cim), **13–15**, 36, 142
Convex, 91
COS, 155
COSIT, 155
Council of Europe, 26–7
cps, 142
CPU, 142
Cray Research, 51, 62, 121
CRT, 65, 142
crystal bistability, 82
CSA, 155–6
CSMA, 38, 113, 142
CUG, 142
Cullinet, 8, 22
cycle time, **18–20**, 160

DASD, 143
database, 8, **21–3**, 24, 32–3, 45, 47, 80, 93, 96–7, 117
database administrator, 24
database management system (DBMS), 21, 22, 24, 32–3, 47, 93, 96–7
(data) communications, 11, 45, 54, 60–61, 68–9, 77–8, 79, 87–8, 89, 95, 101, 110, 113–14, 135, 138–9
data dictionary, **24–5**
Data General, 71
Datapoint, 113
data processing (DP), 43, 49, 62, 71, 76, 79, 80, 91, 120, 128, 143
data protection, **26–7**
Data Protection Act, 26, 27, 39
Data Protection Committee, 26

Data Protection Registrar, 27
Dataquest, 51
Date, Chris, 32
Datel, 68, 138, 139
DBMS (database management system), 21, 22, 24, 32–3, 47, 93, 96–7
DCA, 78, 143
DDL (data description language), 22, 143
DEC (Digital Equipment Corp), 15, 38, 63, 71, 95, 116, 131
declarative language, 76
Dell Computer, 20
Department of Trade & Industry (DTI), 15, 44, 50, 117
departmental computing, 61
design methodologies, **28–9**
desktop publishing (DTP), **30–1**, 118, 144
DIA, 143
diary management, 80
differential analyser, 82
digital data communications, 54–5, 68, 135, 138–9
disc, magnetic, 42, 45, 84, 85, 86, 88, 112, 122–3, 132, 143, 145
disc mirroring, 42
disc, optical, 84–6
distributed database (DDBMS), **32–3**, 143
distributed processing, 61, 79, 102
DML (data manipulation language), 22, 143
DP (data processing), 43, 49, 62, 71, 76, 79, 80, 91, 120, 128, 143
DPM, 143
Dram, 19–20, 144
DTI (Department of Trade & Industry), 15, 44, 50, 117
Du Pont Optical, 86

EBCDIC, 144
ECL, **16–17**, 66, 131, 132, 144
ECLAT, 156
Ecma, 38, 56, 57, 78, 89, 156
ECSA, 156
EDI (electronic data interchange), **34–5**, 117, 144
Edifact, 34, 144
EDP, 79, 144
Edsac, 62, 65
EEC, 35, 36, 37, 55, 82, 83
EFT, 34, 144
EGA, 118, 119, 144
electronic data interchange (EDI), **34–5**, 117, 144
electronic mail, 77, 80, 110, 117, 137, 148
embedded systems, 3
encyclopaedia, 24
Eniac, 62, 65, 128
Eprom, 144
Esprit, 35, **36–7**, 44, 53, 145
ETA Systems, 91
Ethernet, **38**, 58, 67, 113
Eureka, 37
European Optical Bistability Project, 82
Eurosinet, 156
expert systems, 8, **39–40**
Expert Systems International, 39
Expertech, 39

F.200, 12
failsafe systems, 41–2
FAST, 156
fault tolerance, **41–2**, 129
fax, 11, 110, 137
femto (prefix), 160
ferrite core (memory technology), 65, 126
ferrite core disc read-write head, 112
fifth generation, 4, 8, **43–4**, 52, 75–6, 84, 91, 128
file server, **45**
financial modelling, 104, 121
first generation (mainframes), 65
Floating Point Systems, 92
flops, 145

164

Fortran, 3, 46, 49, 75, 101, 121, 145
fourth generation language, 5, 10, **46–7**, 48
fourth generation (mainframes), 66, 91, 126
function point, **48–9**

gallium arsenide (GaAs), 16, **50–51**, 66, 145
gateway, 137
Gb, 145
GCR, 145
GEC Software, 52
Geisco, 35
General Electric (of USA), 65
General Motors, 67
giga (prefix), 160
Government (British), 7, 10, 26, 29, 50, 68, 73–4, 87, 108, 117, 154
graphics, 5, 30, 104, 110, 118, 119, 133
GTDI (Guidelines for Trade Data Interchange), 34
GUIDE, 156

HDA, 145
Helix Expert Systems, 39
Hercules, 118
Heriot-Watt University, 82, 83
Hewlett-Packard, 31, 99
hierarchical database, 22, 96
high level languages, 98
high speed buffer, 20
Honeywell, 65
Honeywell Bull, 42, 71, 121
hypercube, 92

I.420, 54, 55
IBM, 3, 15, 18, 19, 20, 22, 30, 31, 33, 35, 39, 42, 48, 58, 60, 61, 63, 65, 66, 71, 78, 80, 85, 88, 95, 96, 97, 99, 100, 102, 105, 108, 112, 114, 116, 118, 119, 121, 126, 143, 145, 147, 149, 151, 159

IC (integrated circuit), 65, 66, 140, 145
ICL, 5, 15, 16, 35, 65, 68, 70, 71, 78, 88, 99, 120, 126
Icot, 44
IDA, 54, 55, 145
Idea (International Data Exchange Association), 35, 156
IDPM, 156
IEE, 156
IEEE, 38, 56, 89, 95, 113, 116, 156
IFIP, 156
Imperial Software Technology, 52
information engineering, 6, 29
Information Engineering Directorate, 44
information retrieval, 117
information technology (IT), 146
Information Technology Advisory Panel, 87
Information Technology Ltd (ITL), 42
Inland Revenue, 52
Inmos, 92
instruction set, 18, 98–9, 120
Intech, 5
Intel, 16, 38
International Network Services, 35
International Telecommunications Union, 12
I/O, 99, 121, 145
ips, 145
Ipse, 10, **52–3**, 146
IPSS, 135, 146
IRDS, 25, 146
ISDN, **54–5**, 146
ISO, 25, 34, 38, **56–7**, 67, 78, 89, 105, 106, 135, 148, 157
Istel, 35, 117
IT, 146
ITUSA, 157

Jackson, Michael, 28, 29

165

James Martin Associates, 6, 29
Jones, Capers, 49
Josephson, Brian, 108
Josephson junction, 108, 109

Kb, 146
kilo (prefix), 160
Kilostream, 54, 68, 139
knowledge base, 39
knowledge engineering, 8

Lan, 38, 45, **58–9**, 67, 113–14, 146
Learmonth and Burchett, 6, 28
Leo I, 62, 65, 79
Lighthill Report, 7
Linpack, 71
Lips, 146
Lisp, 43, 76
logical unit (LU), 60
Lotus Development Corp, 104
Lovelace, Lady Ada, 4
LSI, 65–6, 126, 130, 146
LU 6.2, **60–61**
J Lyons & Co, 62, 79

magnetic card, 84
magnetic disc, 42, 45, 84, 85, 88, 112, 122–3, 132, 143, 145
magnetic drum, 84
magnetic tape, 16, 84, 145
magnetic tape cassettes, 16
mainframe, 13, 17, 18, 45, 58, **62–4**
mainframe generations, **65–6**, 70, 88, 90, 93, 97, 102, 115, 120, 121, 122, 131, 143
main memory, 19, 20, 43, 65, 66, 91, 92, 126, 127, 144
Manchester University, 65
Map, **67**, 147
Martin, James, 29
Mb, 147
MCA, 147
McDonnell Douglas, 93
MCGA, 119, 147
MDA, 118, 119, 147
mega (prefix), 160

megastream, 54, 68, 139
Meiko, 92
memory access time, 19, 20
memory interleaving, 19
Mercury Communications, **68–9**
mercury delay lines, 65
MHz, 20, 147
micro (computer or processor), 9, 14, 47, 63–4, 74, 115, 141
micro (prefix), 160
Microdata, 93
microfilm, 85, 142
microinstructions, 98
Microprocessor Applications Project, 74
Microsoft, 115
Microsystems Centres, 74
milli (prefix), 160
mini (computer), 9, 14, 18, 58, 63–4, 66, 80, 102, 115, 133
Ministry of Defence, 4, 50
mips, 18, **70–72**, 147
MIS, 147
MITI, 76
MMI, 147
modem, 11, 138
modular programming, 28
Mos, 16, 50, 66, 131, 148
MOTIS, 148
MTBF, 148
MTTR, 148
Mueller, Alex, 108
multiprocessor system, 41, 71, 90
multitasking, 90
multiuser micro, 58, 64, 93, 115

National Computing Centre (NCC), 9, **73–4**, 157
National Council for Civil Liberties, 26
natural language system, 8, 43, 84
nano (prefix), 160
NC (numerical control), 13, 148
NCC (National Computing Centre), 9, **73–4**, 157
NCR, 42, 71

NCube, 92
NCUF, 157
network, 32, 34–5, 38, 45, 54, 58–9, 60, 61, 67, 68–9, 88, 101, 102–3, 110, 113–14, 117, 133, 134, 137, 138, 139
networked database, 22, 96
Nmos, 132, 148
non-procedural language, 43, **75–6**

OCR, 148
ODA, **77–8**, 148
OEM, 148
Oftel, 157
office automation, 36, 38, **79–81**
Olivetti, 78
Open Software Foundation (OSF), 116, 157
operating system, 93–4, 100, 115–16, 141
optical computing, **82–3**
optical disc, **84–6**
optical fibre, 68, 87–8
Oracle (broadcast videotex), 111
Oracle Corp, 22, 32–3, 105
OSI, 56, 67, 77, 81, **89**, 103, 135, 148–9
OSI seven layer model, 67, 77, 89, 135

PABX, 149
packet-switching, 11, 68, 135–6, 138, 149
PAD, 149
parallel processing, 43, 75, **90–2**, 128
PC (personal computer), 14, 18, 19, 20, 21, 30, 31, 38, 39, 47, 58, 62, 64, 66, 74, 80, 86, 93, 97, 104, 114, 118–19, 133, 147, 149
PCB, 130, 149
PCM (plug-compatible manufacturer), 149
PCTE, 4, 53, 149
peer-to-peer communications, 60, 61

performance (of computers), 70–72
personal computer (PC), 14, 18, 19, 20, 21, 30, 31, 38, 39, 47, 58, 62, 64, 66, 74, 80, 86, 93, 97, 104, 114, 118–19, 133, 147, 149
PGA, 149
Philips, 52, 86
physical unit (PU), 60
Pick, **93–4**
Pick, Dick, 93
Pick Forum, 93
Pick Systems, 93
pico (prefix), 160
pipelining, 121
Pitcom, 157
PL/1, 3, 100, 149
plated wire memory, 126
Plessey, 132
port, 63
portable computers, 16
Pos (point of sale), 149
Posix, 116
Post Office, 11
Post Office Work Unit (POWU), 70, 150
Powers Samas, 65
Prestel, 95, 124
Prime, 15
printer, 11, 30, 31, 45
print server, 45
privacy, 26
procedural language, 75
process control, 3, 13, 63, 64, 79, 146
profile, 67
program generator, 46
programming languages, 3–4, 43, 46–7, 52, 75–6, 101
Prolog, 43, 76
Prom, 150
protocol, 35, 60, 67, 89, **95**, 102, 113, 124, 135, 143
protocol converter, 89
PSS, 135, 138, 150
PSTN, 125, 138, 139, 150
PTT, 11, 12, 135, 150

167

Pyramid Technology, 99

query language, 49

Race, 36–7, 150
Ram, 50, 132, 150
Ramp-C, 71
RAS, 150
read/write head, 85, 112, 122, 145
records processing, 80
referential integrity, 105
relational database (RDBMS), 22, 23, 32, 33, **96–7**, 105, 150
Risc, 18, **98–9**, 129, 150–51
robot, 14, 15
Rom, 50, 86, 151
Royal Society, 87
RPG, 47, 100
RS232, 11
RTI (Relational Technology Inc), 22, 32–3

SAA (Systems Application Architecture), 61, **100–101**, 105, 114, 151
Satstream, 139
scalar processing, 120, 121
schema, 22
scientific computing, 43, 49, 62, 79, 91, 99, 120, 128
SD-Scicon, 52
second generation language, 46
second generation (mainframes), 65
Sequel, 105
Sequent, 91
seven layer model (for OSI), 67, 77, 89, 135
semantic database, 23
SERC, 157
shell (for expert system), 39
shell (of Unix), 115
SI units, 160
Siemens, 78
silicon, 16, 50, 51, 65, 66, 130
Sinclair Research, 131, 132
Sitpro, 34, 157

skills shortage, 48, 74
SNA (Systems Network Architecture), 60, 61, 100, 101, **102–3**, 151
software engineering, 3, 9–10, 74
Software Engineering Demonstration Initiative, 10
software productivity, 46, 47, 48–9, 52
Software Products Scheme, 74
Software Tools Demonstration Centre, 10, 74
SPAG, 157
Spectrum Manufacturers Association, 93
Sperry, 71, 131
spreadsheet, 47, 49, 77, 78, 80, **104**
SQL, 101, **105–6**, 151
Sram, 20
SSADM, 29, 151
standby generator, 41
Stanford University, California, 109
STC, 87
Strategic Defence Initiative, 37
Stratus, 42
structured programming, 28, 29
sub-schema, 22
Sun Microsystems, 99, 133
supercomputer, 62, 66, 121
superconductivity, **107–9**
supermini, 17, 62
Sydney Development Corp, 137
System X, 54, 139
systems analysis, 5, 10, 73
Systems Application Architecture (SAA), 61, **100–101**, 105, 114, 151
Systems Network Architecture (SNA), 60, 61, 100, 101, 102–3, 151

Tandem Computers, 41–2, 71
tape, magnetic, 16, 84, 145
TC97, 56
TCM, 151

168

telephone system, 11, 54, 68, 135, 138
teletex, 12, 77, **110–11**, 137
teletext, 111, 125
telex, 11, 77, 110, 137
TEMA, 157–8
tera (prefix), 160
terminal, 5, 11, 16, 32, 45, 58, 60, 83, 90, 95, 102, 110, 124, 125, 133, 135
Texas Instruments, 130
text storage and retrieval, 80
thermionic valves, 65
thin-head film, **112**
third generation language, 46, 47
third generation (mainframes), 65–6
Threshold scheme, 73
timesharing, 104
TMA, 158
token passing, 113
token ring, 58, 67, **113–14**
Top, 67, 151
transactions per hour, 71
transactions per second, 71
transaction processing, 21, 34–5, 41, 96
transistor, 65
Trilogy, 131, 132
TTL, 17, 66, 151

UKCMG, 158
uninterruptible power supply, 41
Unisys, 15, 17, 23, 41, 47, 71
United Nations, 34
Univac, 41
Univac I, 65
Unix, 93, 94, **115–16**
US Department of Defense, 3, 52, 53

V.24, 11

Vanguard, 117
Vans, 34, 117, 152
VAR, 152
VDU, 11, 13, 118–19, 142, 149, 152, 153
VDU standards, **118–19**, 149
vector processing, 18, **120–21**, 129
vertical recording, 112, **122–3**
VGA, 119, 152
videotex, 111, 117, **124–5**
view (in database context), 22
viewdata, 125
VLSI, 66, **126–7**, 131, 152
voice coil motor, 112
von Neumann, John, 128
von Neumann architecture, 75, **128–9**

wait state, 20
Wan (wide area network), 135, 152
Williams tube, 65
Winchester disc, 45, 86, 145
word (unit of measure), 159–60
word processing, 31, 38, 79, 80, 104, 110, 146
workstation, 5, 9, 14, 45, 54, 58, 66, 99, 102, **133–4**
Worm, 85, 152
WSI, **130–32**, 152
Wysiwyg, 153

X.21, 55
X.25, 11, 95, **135–6**
X.400, 77, 110, **137**, 148
Xenix, 115
Xerox, 31, 38
X-Stream, **138–9**

Young, Arthur, 6
Younger Committee, 26
Younger, Kenneth, 26
Yourdon, Ed, 28, 29

COMPUTER WEEKLY PUBLICATIONS

Computer Weekly is the UK's leading weekly computer newspaper which goes to over 112,000 computer professionals each week. Founded in 1967, the paper covers news, reviews and features for the computer industry. In addition, *Computer Weekly* also publishes books relevant to and of interest to its readership.

Publications to date (obtainable through your bookshop or by ringing 01–685–9435/01–661–3050) are:

Considering Computer Contracting? – The Computer Weekly Guide to Becoming a Freelance Computer Professional by Michael Powell

Everybody in the computer industry talks of doubling their salary by going freelance. This book, written by a freelancer, explains how it's done. The topics covered, including how to form your own company, and handling your finance, also make this book useful for people in other industries considering going it alone.

". . .is essential reading for anyone considering taking up contract work."
Guardian

ISBN 1–85384–000–9   156 pages   Price £10.95p

Computer Weekly Book of Puzzlers Compiled by Jim Howson

Test your powers of lateral thinking with this compendium of 187 of the best puzzles over the years in *Computer Weekly*. The detailed explanations of how solutions are reached make this a useful guide to recreational mathematics.

ISBN 1–85384–002–5   162 pages   Price £6.95p

A Simple Guide to Data and Activity Analysis
by Rosemary Rock-Evans

A clear guide, steeped in practical experience in leading user sites, to effective analysis of any organisation and how to represent the results for the computer.

ISBN 1-85384-001-7   c.300 pages   Price £19.95

IT Perspectives Conference: The Future of the IT Industry

Many nuggets of strategic thought are contained in this carefully edited transcript of the actual words spoken by leading IT industry decision makers at Computer Weekly's landmark conference held late in 1987. The conference was dedicated to discussing current and future directions the industry is taking from four perspectives: supplier perspectives; communications perspectives; user perspectives and future perspectives.

ISBN 1-85384-008-4   224 pages   Price £45

Open Systems: The Basic Guide to OSI and its Implementation
by Peter Judge

We recognise the need for a concise, clear guide to the complex area of computer standards, untrammeled by jargon and with appropriate comprehensible analogies to simplify this difficult topic. This book, a unique collaboration between *Computer Weekly* and the magazine *Systems International*, steers an independent and neutral path through this contentious area and is essential for users and suppliers and is required reading for all who come into contact with the computer industry.

ISBN 1-85384-009-2   192 pages   Price £12.95

The Computer Weekly Annual Guide to Resources '89

This extensively indexed book fulfils the computer industry's need for an independent, handy up-to-date reference review signposting and interpreting the key trends in the computer industry and how companies and their products are adapting to them. A key section is an in-depth independent discussion of 200 software and supplier companies, and of leading industry sectors and significant new products.

ISBN 1-85384-014-9   352 pages   Price £45

Aliens Guide to the Computer Industry by John Kavanagh

In a lucid and light style, leading computer industry writer John Kavanagh discusses how the various parts of the computer industry inter-relate and what makes it tick. Complete with extensive index, the book is invaluable for all who come into contact with the computer industry.

ISBN 1–85384–012–2   192 pages   Price £9.95

How to Get Jobs in Microcomputing by John F Charles

As micros proliferate throughout organisations, opportunities for getting jobs in the micro area are expanding rapidly. The author, who has worked with micros in major organisations, discusses how to get started in microcomputing, describes the different types of job available, and offers tips and hints based on practical experience. Ideal for recent graduates, and those already working with minicomputers or mainframes, who are looking towards a career in micros.

ISBN 1–85384–010–6   160 pages   Price £6.95

Women in Computing by Judith Morris

Written by an experienced editor of several computer magazines, this book reflects the upsurge in awareness of the important role which women can play in helping to stem the critical skills shortage within the computer industry. The book addresses women's issues in a practical and sensible way, and is aimed at all businesswomen who work in the computer industry or with computers.

ISBN 1–85384–004–1   c.160 pages   Price £9.95

Selling Information Technology: A Practical Career Guide by Eric Johnson

Selling in IT requires more skill and creativity than selling in any other profession. This essential handbook for IT sales people explains why and provides practical down-to-earth advice on achieving the necessary extra skills. A collaboration between *Computer Weekly* and the National Computing Centre, this book discusses practical career issues, general IT sales issues, and key industry developments.

ISBN 1–85012–684–3   264 pages   Price £12.50